What's Math all about?

Everything!

Alex Frith,
Minna Lacey
& Lisa Jane Gillespie

Illustrated by Adam Larkum

Designed by Ruth Russell,
Anna Gould and Hannah Ahmed

Math consultants:
Jeff Hebert and Giles Dickins
Edited by Rosie Dickins
US editors: Carrie Armstrong & Sabrina Ripp

Contents

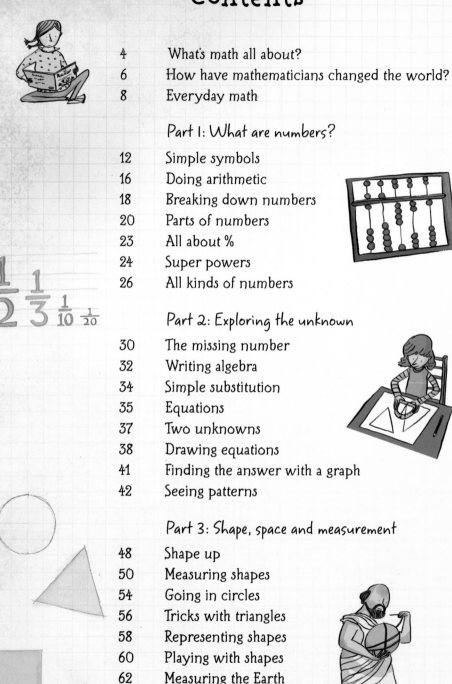

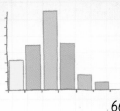

Part 4: Facts and figures

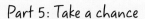

Part 5: Take a chance

Part 6: More about math

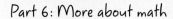

Internet links

You can find out lots more about math on the internet – you can read about different types of numbers, examine theorems, analyze statistics or construct your own graphs. For links to these websites, and many more, go to **www.usborne-quicklinks.com** and type in the keywords **what is math**.

The links are regularly reviewed and updated, but Usborne Publishing cannot be responsible for any website other than its own. Please follow the internet safety guidelines displayed on the Usborne Quicklinks Website.

What's math all about?

You might think math is all about numbers. It is — but it's also about shapes, amounts and patterns. Numbers provide a way to measure shapes, count things and even recognize patterns.

Math is used to find answers to questions, such as how long a new bridge should be, or who is most likely to win a game. Even complex things, such as the flight patterns of birds, can be turned into mathematical models. Models help people make predictions about what will happen in the future.

Who does math?

Everyone does math, all the time. You use math to make a cake, decide how much food to buy for a party or plan what move to make in a game.

Math is also a way of thinking and working things out that you can apply to any activity, even solving picture puzzles.

It's all Greek

The word 'mathematics' comes from the Greek word *mathema*, meaning learning, study or science.

Understanding the question

Sometimes the hardest thing about solving a math problem isn't the *numbers*, but the *words*.

Part of the knack of math is reading questions carefully. For example: how many months have 28 days?

One. February.

Wrong! *Every* month has 28 days. It's just that most months have 2 or 3 more days on top of that.

This is a picture sudoku puzzle. To complete the puzzle, draw the correct face into each space in the grid.

Every row, every column and every 4-square box in the grid has to include one picture of each face...

...and each face can only appear ONCE in each row, column or box.

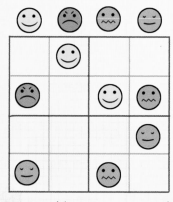

There are no numbers in this puzzle, but to solve it you have to think logically. This is an important skill in lots of branches of math.

(The answer is on page 93.)

One step at a time

A lot of math boils down to knowing how to set out information in a clear way. To solve a problem, mathematicians use skills similar to a detective. They look at the evidence or the facts, then apply reasoning to lead from one step to the next, until they find the answer. Here's an example:

How many blue marbles are in the box?

Fact 1:
The box contains only red and blue marbles.

Fact 2:
There are 10 marbles in total.

Fact 3:
There are 3 red marbles.

$10 - 3 = 7$
I deduce there are 7 blue marbles in the box.

What's the point of math?

Numbers aren't exactly real 'things', but the things they describe are real. For example, you can have two dogs, or two apples, but 'two' on its own doesn't really describe anything. Some math is about real things, but lots of math is about unreal, or abstract, ideas.

Abstract, or **pure**, math is often about exploring patterns and tackling puzzles. It doesn't always have a use in everyday life. But learning pure math teaches you how to think in a certain way.

Sometimes, even the most obscure math facts turn out to have a practical use. Turn the page to find out how people have used math to change the world...

Can you prove it?

To solve problems, mathematicians don't just do calculations in their heads and write down the answer. A big part of doing math is explaining *how* they got the answer.

I'm thinking of a number. I double it, then add another 6. If the answer is 16, what was the number I first thought of?

5

How did you work that out?

I started at 16 and worked backwards. 6 less than 16 is 10. Half of 10 is 5. So you must have started with the number 5.

How have mathematicians changed the world?

Mathematicians have experimented with numbers and ideas for centuries. This has led to some remarkable discoveries that have changed our lives, often by accident.

Understanding the universe

In the early 17th century, German mathematician and astronomer Johannes Kepler experimented with shapes and worked out how the planets and the Sun relate to each other. He came up with the theory that planets orbit the Sun in elliptical (or oval) – not circular – paths. His discoveries helped later astronomers to predict how planets and their moons move through space.

Art and perspective

For thousands of years, artists struggled to draw distances between objects accurately. In the 15th century, Italian engineer Brunelleschi found a trick: to show distance, he drew two lines that met at a point on the horizon, representing parallel lines, such as the sides of a street.

Look at the picture below to see how it works:

Computer language

19th-century British mathematician George Boole invented Boolean logic – a system of giving values to statements. In his system, a statement is given a value of '1' if it is true, or '0' if it is false. Boolean logic became the basis for the way computers work.

The sides of a real street are parallel – they never meet.

The sides of the street in this picture aren't parallel, but the street looks as if it goes into the distance.

Strong arches

Bridges are often supported by arches. The shape of an arch allows the weight of the bridge to be spread out along the arch to supports at each end, instead of pushing down in the middle.

Ancient Roman mathematicians were among the first to use this design to build huge bridges and aqueducts.

Square bridge

Arched bridge

The weight of each stone pushes straight down.

The weight of each stone is spread out.

Rocket science

To make a rocket, engineers need to work out many things, including the best launch path, how much fuel the rocket will need, and how fast it must travel to escape the earth's gravity.

Many of these calculations are based on laws of force and motion discovered by 17th-century British mathematician and physicist Isaac Newton.

Maps and surveys

A new system for finding places on maps was invented by French mathematician René Descartes in the 17th century. In his system, any point on a map can be described by its distance along a horizontal line (the x-axis) and a vertical line (the y-axis) from a particular point.

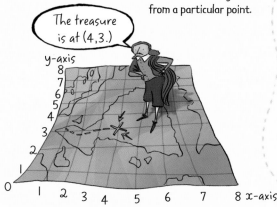

The treasure is at (4,3.)

This is known as the system of Cartesian coordinates. Coordinates are found on country maps, road maps, archaeological plans, computer charts and even treasure maps.

Searching the internet

In the USA in the late 20th century, computer scientists Larry Page and Sergey Brin used a kind of math called optimization to build a tool for searching the internet.

Their original tool was meant to search through scientific papers to find out which ones discussed each other's findings. But the project soon grew, and became the basis for the internet search website known as *Google*.

Everyday math

You learn lots of math without ever opening a book. In fact there are many types of math that you might do every day – not just at school – without even thinking of them as math.

Watching a tournament

Whenever someone wins a medal at a tournament, such as the Olympic Games, it's recorded on a medals table. Understanding the information on the table is a type of math.

This country has the most gold medals.

This country has the most medals overall.

Country	Gold	Silver	Bronze
Canada	14	7	5
Germany	10	13	7
USA	9	15	13
Norway	9	8	6
South Korea	6	6	2

Baking cupcakes

To bake a cake, you need to measure out all the ingredients, mix them up in the right order, and bake them for the right amount of time. Measuring quantities is part of math. If the recipe makes 12 cupcakes, but you want to make 18, you'll have to do even more math.

All birds can fly.

Penguins can't fly.

Maybe they're not really birds, then!

Or maybe it's just not true that ALL birds can fly.

Winning an argument

Some people try to win arguments by shouting the loudest. But there's another way – using logical reasoning, which is a type of math, too.

Planning a route

Imagine you're going on a trip, and you have to pick up ten friends in a minivan. You'll need to use a type of math to work out the most efficient route to get to each house, without going back on your tracks too often.

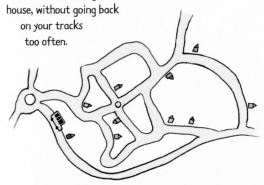

Wrapping a present

Wrapping paper usually comes in long rolls. But you don't need all the paper to wrap a small present. To cut out the correct amount of paper, most people estimate how much to use – a very important part of math.

Waking up in the morning

How do you decide what time to set your alarm clock for? You might need to work out how much time it takes to bathe, dress and eat your breakfast before you're ready to leave the house. Even if you only guess the answers, this is all math.

Planning a party

When you invite lots of friends to a party, you need to do some math to make sure you have enough food and drinks. If it's a sleep-over, you might have to rearrange your bedroom so there's enough room for everyone – another type of math.

5 friends

5 bottles of lemonade

3 pizzas with 8 slices; everyone gets 4 slices each, with 4 left over.

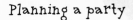

Part 1:
What are numbers?

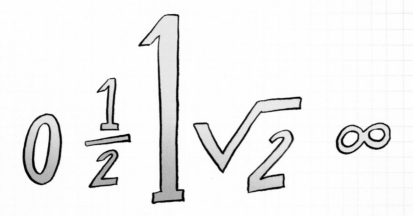

Numbers were invented to help people count and measure things. But they have a life of their own, too. Mathematicians have discovered that the way numbers are connected creates all sorts of patterns. Sometimes these patterns reveal useful tricks that help with counting and measuring things, but sometimes they're just patterns.

Simple symbols

Most numbers can be written using just ten symbols, or **digits**: 0, 1, 2, 3, 4, 5, 6, 7, 8 and 9. These are sometimes called Hindu-Arabic numerals, because they're based on symbols first used in India, and later the Arab world, over a thousand years ago.

Natural numbers

If you start at 1, and count up one at a time, you're counting **natural numbers**. Natural numbers describe how many of something you're referring to, such as one fish, or two bottles.

The symbol '0', or **zero**, is an exception – it stands for not having any at all. Using just ten digits, it's possible to describe any natural number, no matter how big it is. This is thanks to the digit zero...

Zero to the rescue

Zero lets you leave gaps in numbers. For example, 5 and 6 can be used to write 5, 6, 56 or 65. But introducing a 0 lets you write 50, 60, 506, 605, 560 and 650. The important part is the position of the zero, and the number of zeroes there are.

If you want to count your toes, the digits 1 to 9 will get you most of the way. To count the final, tenth, toe you use two digits: 1 followed by 0. The 1 doesn't stand for *one toe* any more, but for *one group of ten toes*, while the 0 stands for *no extra toes*.

Counting and writing

One of the first things people needed to count was probably the number of animals they kept. They kept track of amounts by carving groups of strokes called *tallies* onto wood or bone.

Ancient bones with tally markings are some of the oldest forms of writing ever found.

One, another one, another one...

Celebrity number

Over 1,500 years ago, people in Asia and Central America used various different symbols to represent 'nothing'.

The ring shape, 0, was invented nearly 1,400 years ago in India. It was used by an Indian scholar named Brahmagupta to help write out really big numbers.

One group of ten 10 No extra parts

Counting in tens

Counting in tens is the basis for a way of counting called the **decimal system**, from the Latin *decem*, meaning 'ten'. It's also known as **base 10**.

In the decimal system, the position of each digit shows its value, such as 'hundreds,' 'tens' or 'units'.

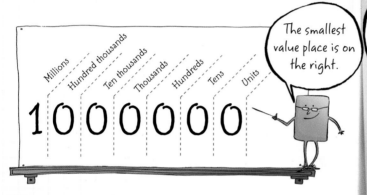

The smallest value place is on the right.

Millions · Hundred thousands · Ten thousands · Thousands · Hundreds · Tens · Units

1 0 0 0 0 0 0

When you see a big number written out, you can figure out what each digit is worth from where it sits, known as its **place value**. Here are two examples:

This number is called 'Two thousand, one hundred and thirty-six'.

2 thousands · 1 hundred · 3 tens · 6 units

2 1 3 6

Really big numbers are often written with commas or spaces, to make it easier to work out which column each digit is in.

This number is called 'Five hundred million, ninety-seven thousand, eight hundred and thirty'.

5 0 0 , 0 9 7 , 8 3 0

Binary code

Counting in tens isn't the only way to count. Computers use a counting system with just two digits, 0 and 1. This is known as binary code.

There are 10 kinds of people in the world... ...those who understand binary code, and those who don't.

Each 0 represents a switch that is turned off in the computer's hardware, and 1 represents a switch that's turned on. A switch can't be in any other position, so there's no need to use more than two digits. In binary, the number 2 is expressed as '10': one group of 'twos', and no 'ones'.

Roman counting

Ancient Romans used symbols that we now call Roman numerals. I, II, III, IV, V, VI, VII, VIII, IX and X stood for the numbers 1 to 10. They didn't have a zero, so they had to keep inventing new symbols to stand for big numbers.

L = 50   C = 100
D = 500   M = 1,000

It took lots of Roman numerals to write a big number such as 1,808: MDCCCVIII.

Negative numbers

You can also count backwards starting from zero. Numbers less than zero are called negative numbers. The number written -1 is properly called 'negative one,' although it's often called 'minus one.'

The idea of negative numbers may seem strange, but they can describe things in the real world. For example, if you owe a friend $5, but don't have any money, you could say that you have $-5, or 'negative five dollars.'

Negative problems

The first book to describe how to use negative numbers was written in Ancient China over 2,000 years ago.

It's called *Nine Chapters on the Mathematical Art* and explains how to use negative numbers to solve problems.

Forever and ever

If you start counting up from zero, you could keep going and never reach a final number. You can always add 1 to a positive number to get a bigger number. There's no such thing as 'the biggest number', but there is a word to represent the *idea* of such a number: **infinity**. It's represented by the symbol ∞ .

Infinity is an abstract idea that doesn't represent anything that really exists. For example, the number of grains of sand in a desert, or stars in a galaxy, may be incredibly large — but it isn't infinite.

Endless sign

Mathematician John Wallis introduced the symbol ∞ to stand for infinity in 1655.

If you trace the symbol with a pencil, you can keep going around and around forever. It was also an easy symbol to use in printing, as it was made by just putting an 8 on its side.

An infinity paradox

19th-century German mathematician Georg Cantor explored different ways to reach infinity, and found an interesting pair of facts...

Let A be a set of numbers: all the natural numbers.

1, 2, 3, 4, 5....

This set is infinite.

Let B be another set of numbers: all the even numbers.

2, 4, 6, 8, 10...

This set is also infinite.

Imagine two people counting out each set in unison:

A: 1, 2, 3, 4, 5....
B: 2, 4, 6, 8, 10...

Both sets have the same amount of numbers.

But set A contains all the odd numbers as well as the even numbers. **This means set A is bigger than set B.**

This is an example of a **paradox**: two statements which are both true but also contradict each other.

Alternative counting systems

Long ago, people developed all sorts of counting systems. Some are still in use today.

Symbols and spaces

About 5,000 years ago in Babylonia, where Iraq is today, people counted in 60s. They used 59 different symbols for the numbers 1-59 and left a space for zero. For bigger numbers, each symbol's position stood for groups of 60s, or 60x60s, and so on.

This represents 2,327. The Ancient Egyptians read from right to left and had separate symbols for 2,000, 300, 20 and 7.

This number is 72. The first symbol stands for one group of 60. The next three symbols represent 12 units.

This counting system survives in the way hours are divided into 60 minutes, and minutes into 60 seconds.

Zeroless Egyptians

Around 6,000 years ago, the Ancient Egyptians began to develop a number system using signs for 1-9. They didn't have a way to show zero, so they had to use different symbols to stand for groups of 10s, 100s and so on, as the Romans did.

Numerals and columns

Over 3,000 years ago the Maya people in Central America counted in 20s. They had numerals for 0-19. For bigger numbers, they wrote rows of numerals. The higher rows stood for groups of 20s and 20x20s, like our 10s and 100s.

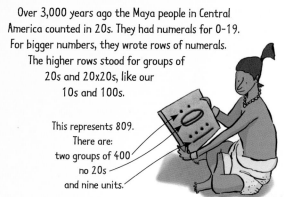

This represents 809. There are: two groups of 400 no 20s and nine units.

Counting with an abacus

There are many versions of an ancient counting tool called an **abacus** – some still in use in parts of Asia today. Each abacus has columns of beads, laid out in a grid. Every column stands for increasing quantities, for example units, 10s, 100s and so on, in the decimal system.

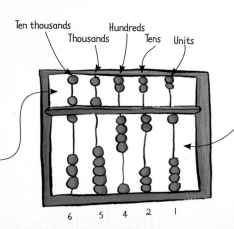

Ten thousands
Thousands
Hundreds
Tens
Units

This abacus shows the number 65,421.

In the lower section, every bead pushed to the top adds 1.

In the upper section, each bead pushed down adds 5.

6   5   4   2   1

Doing arithmetic

Perhaps the most common use for numbers is to do a kind of math called **arithmetic**. Arithmetic combines numbers together using four operations: addition, subtraction, multiplication and division.

Most people use simple arithmetic every day, for example adding up coins to pay for something, or working out how to divide a cake fairly.

Get the order right

Often, the quickest way to solve a problem is to use a calculator. But a calculator won't give you the right answer unless you enter the problem correctly. There's a correct order for solving any arithmetic problem. Here it is:

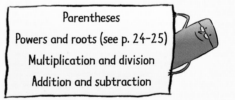

Parentheses
Powers and roots (see p. 24–25)
Multiplication and division
Addition and subtraction

Parentheses show which part of a calculation is meant to be done first. For example, consider 8 + 12 ÷ 4 − 2:

Got it! 16.

Hold on! I haven't even typed the first number.

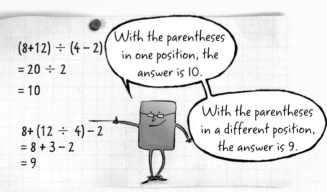

$(8+12) \div (4-2)$
$= 20 \div 2$
$= 10$

With the parentheses in one position, the answer is 10.

$8 + (12 \div 4) - 2$
$= 8 + 3 - 2$
$= 9$

With the parentheses in a different position, the answer is 9.

Guess what?

Sometimes, it's useful to **estimate**, or guess, the answer to a problem. For example, if you're shopping and want to know if you have enough money to buy everything you want, you can **round up** or **round down** the prices to numbers that you can add quickly in your head. This will give you an approximate answer.

> 18 tickets, please.

> Ticket price: $22

> How much for three DVDs?

> A little under $30.

$9.99

$9.99

(Exact answer: $29.97)

If you need to do a calculation quickly, such as 18 x 22, you can just round the numbers to 20 x 20. This problem is easier to do, and will give you an approximate answer that will be close to the exact answer.

20 x 20 = 400

(Exact answer: 18 x 22 = 396)

Guesstimates

Most estimates are made by rounding off *known* numbers. But sometimes it's useful to guess at an answer even if you don't know the numbers. This is often called a **guesstimate**.

Do aliens exist?

American astrophysicist Frank Drake wanted to work out how likely it is there are any alien civilzations in our galaxy. To help answer this big question, he came up with a list of smaller questions. Some of the answers can be estimated through observation, others require guesswork.

Questions that can be estimated:
a) How many stars are there in the galaxy?
b) How many stars have planets?
c) How many planets support life?

Questions that can be guesstimated:
a) How many planets might actually develop life?
b) How many planets might develop civilizations?

> Even using very low guesses to answer each question, there could still be about four thousand civilizations in our galaxy.

Breaking down numbers

Numbers can be broken down into one or more **factors** – numbers that divide exactly into them. Every whole number shares one factor: 1. But most numbers have other factors, too. For instance, 6 has factors 1, 2, 3 and 6.

Finding factors

To find all the factors of a number, try dividing it by every smaller number: 1, 2, 3, 4 and so on. For example, the factors of 24 are:

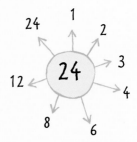

There aren't really any shortcuts to finding factors. But you can make the job quicker by listing them in pairs, starting from 1 and working up.

Number friends

Ancient Greek mathematician Pythagoras founded a community called the Pythagorean Order. Its members believed numbers could explain everything in the world.

Two numbers they especially liked were 220 and 284. If you add up the factors of 220 (except 1 and 220), you get 284.

And if you add up the factors of 284 (except 1 and 284), it makes 220.

Because they shared this strange link, Pythagoreans called them 'amicable numbers'. They symbolized friendship.

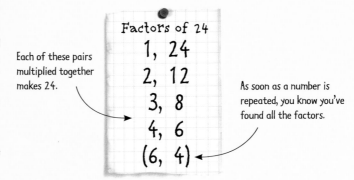

Factors of 24

1, 24
2, 12
3, 8
4, 6
(6, 4)

Each of these pairs multiplied together makes 24.

As soon as a number is repeated, you know you've found all the factors.

Using factors

If you want to solve calculations containing big numbers, it helps to break the numbers down into their factors. For example, to figure out 24 x 3, you could change 24 into a factor pair, such as 3 x 8. Now all you have to figure out is 3 x 3 x 8. This becomes 9 x 8, which is easy if you know your times tables. (The answer is 72.)

Prime numbers

Some numbers have just two factors – themselves and the number 1. These are called **prime numbers**. (The number 1 has only one factor – itself – so it *isn't* considered a prime number.)

You can see which numbers are prime by drawing them out like this...

Non-prime numbers make rectangles.

Prime numbers can only make rectangles if they're all in a line.

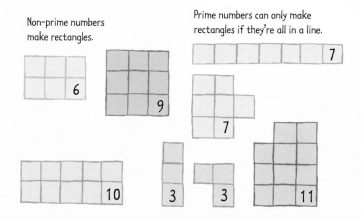

Primes and secrets

In the 1970s, a group of three US math professors, known together as RSA, showed how prime numbers could be used to build uncrackable codes. The RSA method is now used to make online banking and shopping secure.

The trick is to pick two very big prime numbers and multiply them together. This creates one very, very long number. This number can then be combined with a credit card number, so keeping it hidden.

The only known way to retrieve the credit card number is with the original primes. A computer testing every possible combination of known prime numbers would take decades to work out the answer.

Prime puzzle

One of the strange things about prime numbers is that if you write them down in a list, they don't seem to form any pattern.

For thousands of years, mathematicians around the world have been trying to discover a pattern or rule to explain the sequence of prime numbers – without success.

2 3 5 7 11 13 17 19
23 29 31 37 41 43
47 53 59 61 67 71
73 79 83 89 97 101

Parts of numbers

As well as whole numbers, there are also parts of numbers, known as **fractions**. Fractions exist in the real world, too — for example, slices of a cake are fractions.

The number on top of the line is called the **numerator**. This is the number of 'parts.'.

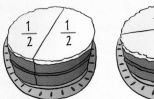
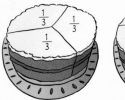

The number below the line is called the **denominator**. This is the total number of 'parts' that make a whole number.

Mixed-up fractions

Proper fractions have a smaller numerator than denominator, such as $\frac{9}{20}$, (nine twentieths). These are the types of fractions you will come across most often.

An **improper fraction** has a larger numerator than denominator. This sort of fraction can also be written as a mixture of whole numbers and proper fractions, called a **mixed number**. Here's an example:

To convert this improper fraction, solve $72 \div 5$.

$$\frac{72}{5} = 14\frac{2}{5}$$

$72 \div 5 = 14$ with a remainder of 2. Or, 14 and $\frac{2}{5}$.

Arty math

When artists draw a person, they often split the body up into fractions. This helps them check that each part is in proportion.

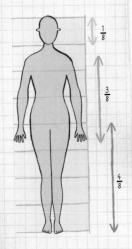

Head = $\frac{1}{8}$ of the total height

Arms = $\frac{3}{8}$ of the total height

Legs = $\frac{4}{8}$ of the total height

Invisible fractions

Whole numbers can be written as fractions, too. For example, the number 2 can be written as $\frac{2}{1}$, meaning 'two oneths'. The '1' at the bottom is known as 'the invisible denominator' because you don't usually write it down.

It's the same number

There are many ways to write the same quantity in fractions. For example $\frac{50}{100}$, $\frac{10}{20}$ and $\frac{1}{2}$ are all different ways of describing a half.

When doing arithmetic, it's often easier to simplify any fractions first. But if you're describing something real, such as the number of people in a glee club who are left-handed, it might be more meaningful to say '5 out of 30,' rather than simplify to '1 out of 6.'

The smallest fraction

If you kept cutting a loaf of bread into smaller and smaller fractions, the slices would soon crumble. Ancient Greek philosophers came up with the idea that if you keep cutting an object in half, you eventually get something so tiny it can't be cut again. They named this imaginary thing an 'atom', which means 'uncuttable' in Ancient Greek.

What's the thinnest slice I can cut, I wonder...

But in the world of math, there are no limits. You can take any number, no matter how small, and divide it in half to get an even smaller number. Just as there is no such thing as the biggest number, only the idea of infinity or ∞, so there is no such thing as the smallest number, only the concept $\frac{1}{\infty}$.

Equal fractions

Whenever you have a fraction, check to see if the numbers above and below the line have common factors – numbers that divide into both of them. If they do, the fraction can be simplified.

For example, look at the fraction $\frac{18}{24}$.

18 and 24 can both be divided by 6.

There are 3 sixes in 18, and 4 sixes in 24.

So $\frac{18}{24}$ is the same as $\frac{3}{4}$.

Shrinking fractions

Increasing the value of the denominator shrinks a fraction. If the numerator stays the same, but the denominator gets bigger, the fraction gets smaller. So $\frac{1}{3}$ is smaller than $\frac{1}{2}$, $\frac{1}{6}$ is even smaller, and $\frac{1}{10}$ is smaller still.

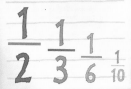

Get the point?

Parts of numbers can be written as decimals as well as fractions, using a dot called a **decimal point**. For example, 0.1 represents a tenth, or the fraction $\frac{1}{10}$. Each position after a decimal point is called a decimal place (d.p.) The first position after the point represents tenths. The second position represents hundredths – and so on.

10ths 100ths 1,000ths 10,000ths

$$0.1\ 4\ 8\ 9$$

Decimal point

This number is written to 4 d.p.

As a fraction, this number would be written $\frac{1,489}{10,000}$.

To multiply a decimal by 10, shift each digit across one column to the left. So, 0.1489 becomes 1.489. To divide 0.1489 by 10, shift each digit one place to the right, and introduce a zero. So, 0.1489 becomes 0.01489.

Comparing stuff

Fractions can be used to compare different amounts of things. Another way of doing this is with a pair of numbers called a **ratio**. For example, imagine you and a friend did a job, but you think you did more work...

If you worked three times as hard as your friend, you could express this with the ratio 3:1. It means for every three parts of work you did, your friend did one.

To express this in fractions, you'd say he did $\frac{1}{4}$ of the work and you did $\frac{3}{4}$.

Making decimals

To turn a fraction into a decimal, solve the division problem described by the fraction. For example, $\frac{1}{2}$ becomes $1 \div 2$, which is 0.5.

On and on and on

Some numbers behave better as fractions than as decimals. $\frac{1}{3}$ is a simple fraction. But as a decimal, $1 \div 3$ leaves you with 0.3333333333333... The 3s go on forever. This number can be shown with a dash above the repeating number, like this: $0.\overline{3}$. It's called 'zero point three recurring'.

A recipe ratio

Ratios are often used on food or drink labels:

Mix 1 part concentrated fruit juice with 5 parts water.

All about %

The symbol %, or **percent**, means 'per 100', or 'out of 100'. A percentage is a kind of fraction that people use for all sorts of things, from exam results and savings rates to sale prices and measurements.

For example, if 35 out of 100 wall tiles are green, you can say that $\frac{35}{100}$, or 35%, are green.

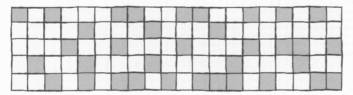

You can use percentages to describe any fraction. You just need to convert the fraction so that it has a denominator of 100.

If 4 students out of a class of 20 have red hair, what percentage have red hair?

One way to get the answer is to imagine how many redheads you'd have if there were 100 students:

1. If there were 5 classes of 20 students, that would give 100 students in total.

2. If 4 in each class have red hair, then the total number of redheads would be 4 x 5, which is 20.

3. So the percentage of redheads in the original class is 20 out of 100, or 20%.

Huh. Only four of us have red hair.

Wow! As many as 20% of us have red hair!

All the same

Sometimes two numbers can look different when they're actually just different ways of describing the same thing.

How much of this circle is blue?

0.5

50% $\frac{1}{2}$

These are all correct ways to answer the question.

Fractions to percent

You can change any fraction into a percentage – just multiply by 100.

To write $\frac{3}{10}$ as a percentage:

$\frac{3}{10}$ x 100 = $\frac{3}{10}$ x $\frac{100}{1}$

= $\frac{300}{10}$

300 ÷ 10 = 30, so $\frac{3}{10}$ is 30%

Roman levy

Using fractions of 100 has been common since Roman times. Roman Emperor Augustus introduced a tax of *centesima rerum venalium*, which meant $\frac{1}{100}$ or 1%, on all goods sold at auction.

This is nothing compared to modern auction houses, which can charge the seller as much as 15% for every item sold.

Order, order!

Mathematicians sometimes talk about **orders of magnitude**. This is a way of comparing the size of numbers. For example 1,000 is one order of magnitude bigger than 100. 10,000 is three orders of magnitude bigger than 10. Every extra zero means one extra order of magnitude.

Rock kestrel: 33cm tall

Elephant 3.3m tall

3.3m = 330cm (see page 51). 330cm is one order of magnitude bigger than 33cm.

Small powers

Any number raised to the power 1 means simply 'one amount of that number.' So, for example, $6^1 = 6$.

Any number to the power -1 becomes a fraction of itself, known as a **reciprocal**. For example, $6^{-1} = \frac{1}{6}$.

Any number raised to the power zero means 'one amount of that number divided by itself'. The answer is always 1. For example, $6^0 = 1$.

Super powers

One of the quickest ways to make a small number grow into a really big number is by using **powers**.

Raising a number to the power 2, for example, means multiplying the number by itself. This is also called **squaring** the number. If you raise 2 to the power 2, you get two squared, which can be written like this: 2^2.

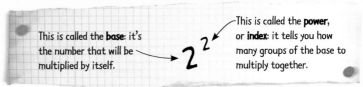

This is called the **base**: it's the number that will be multiplied by itself.

This is called the **power**, or **index**: it tells you how many groups of the base to multiply together.

The answer, 4, is called a **square number**.

If you raise a number to the power 3, you multiply it by itself, then by itself again. This is called **cubing** and creates a **cube number**. For example, 2^3 is 2 x 2 x 2 = 8.

Two squares together make a rectangle, so 2 is not a square number.

4 is a square number because you can use four small squares to make one big square.

8 is a cube number because you can use 8 blocks to make a cube.

Powerful stuff

You can raise a number to any power using a base and an index — it's a useful shorthand for writing out very big numbers. For example, 8 to the power 6 is 8x8x8x8x8x8 = 262,144. But it's much neater to write 8^6.

Powers of 10

Really big numbers are often written in **scientific notation**, which means the base number is 10. For example, you can write 2,310,000 as 2.31×10^6. Each extra power of 10 increases the index by one, and moves each digit one place to the left.

Scientists use scientific notation to help them deal with vast numbers – such as estimating the number of stars in space (roughly 5×10^{22}), or the number of molecules in a teaspoon of water (roughly 1.65×10^{23}).

I'd say there are about 50,000,000, 000,000,000,000, 000 stars up there.

You mean 5×10^{22} stars?

Tiny and huge

Scientists often need to use very large or very small numbers. To write them, they use scientific notation.

To write a really tiny number, they use negative powers of 10. For example,

0.002 becomes 2×10^{-3}

0.00000000006 becomes 6×10^{-11}. (The negative power number tells you the position of the number in d.p.)

To describe large numbers, you can use names as well as this notation. For example:

A decillion = 10^{33}

A vigintillion = 10^{63}

A googol = 10^{100}

A googolplex = $10^{10^{100}}$

Written in full, a googolplex would be a one followed by a googol zeroes – a number so long there's not enough paper in the world to write it on, even in the tiniest writing.

Getting to the root

The opposite of squaring a number is finding its **square root**. This is a number that you can multiply by itself to equal the original number. The square root symbol is $\sqrt{\ }$. The square root of 9, for example, is 3. This is because if you multiply 3 by itself, it equals 9.

You can also find cube roots, $\sqrt[3]{\ }$. A **cube root** is a number that can be cubed to equal the original number. $\sqrt[3]{27} = 3$, because $3 \times 3 \times 3 = 27$. You can also have $\sqrt[4]{\ }, \sqrt[5]{\ }, \sqrt[100]{\ }$ – or any other root.

Two solutions:

If you multiply two negative numbers together, they make a positive number. This fact means a number can have two different square roots.

For example, $2^2 = 4$, and $-2^2 = 4$. So the answer to the question 'what number, when squared, is 4?' is ±2.

25

All kinds of numbers

Some kinds of numbers are useful for describing things in the world. Some are useful to help solve math problems. And some are ideas that mathematicians have invented. Here's a reminder of some common kinds of numbers, and an introduction to some of the weirder ones.

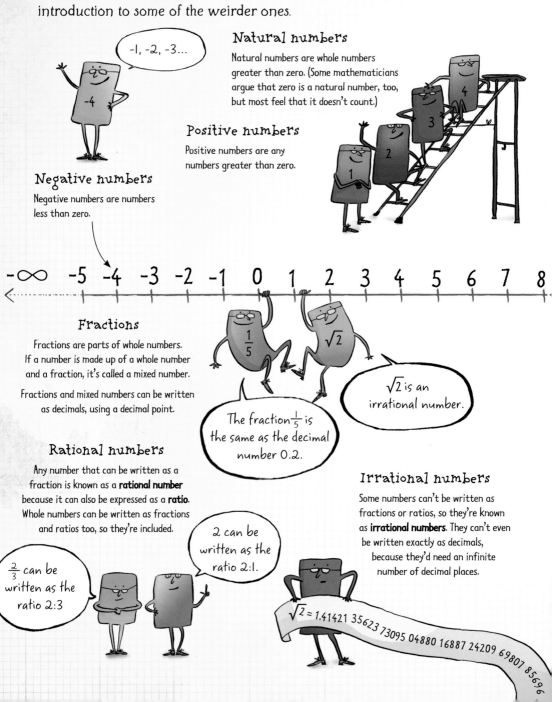

-1, -2, -3...

Natural numbers

Natural numbers are whole numbers greater than zero. (Some mathematicians argue that zero is a natural number, too, but most feel that it doesn't count.)

Positive numbers

Positive numbers are any numbers greater than zero.

Negative numbers

Negative numbers are numbers less than zero.

$-\infty$ -5 -4 -3 -2 -1 0 1 2 3 4 5 6 7 8

Fractions

Fractions are parts of whole numbers. If a number is made up of a whole number and a fraction, it's called a mixed number.

Fractions and mixed numbers can be written as decimals, using a decimal point.

The fraction $\frac{1}{5}$ is the same as the decimal number 0.2.

$\sqrt{2}$ is an irrational number.

Rational numbers

Any number that can be written as a fraction is known as a **rational number** because it can also be expressed as a **ratio**. Whole numbers can be written as fractions and ratios too, so they're included.

2 can be written as the ratio 2:1.

$\frac{2}{3}$ can be written as the ratio 2:3

Irrational numbers

Some numbers can't be written as fractions or ratios, so they're known as **irrational numbers**. They can't even be written exactly as decimals, because they'd need an infinite number of decimal places.

$\sqrt{2}$ = 1.41421 35623 73095 04880 16887 24209 69807 85696

Perfect numbers

Some numbers have a special property. If you take all the number's factors (except for the number itself), you find that they add up to make that number. The factors of 6 are 1, 2, 3 and 6. 1 + 2 + 3 = 6, so 6 is a **perfect number**. The next perfect number is 28. So far, 47 perfect numbers have been found.

Factors and primes

Factors are whole numbers that divide exactly into a bigger whole number. Some numbers only have two factors, themselves and 1. These are called prime numbers.

One billion, one billion and one, one billion and two…

Infinity

If you could keep counting forever and ever, you would never finish. The word that expresses this idea is infinity.

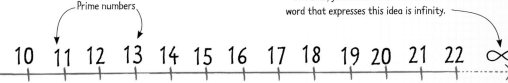

Prime numbers

9 10 11 12 13 14 15 16 17 18 19 20 21 22 ∞

Imaginary numbers

If you multiply two negative numbers together, you always create a positive number. This means that no negative numbers have a real square root.

But mathematicians decided to invent a new kind of number based on finding $\sqrt{-1}$, which is represented by the symbol i. These numbers are called **imaginary numbers**. Unlike any real number, you won't find imaginary numbers on the number line.

I get it, $i^2 = -1$.

Real numbers

Real numbers are all the points on the number line. Any position you can point to represents a real number. They can be positive or negative, fractions or decimals, they include zero, rational and even irrational numbers.

$\frac{1}{3}$ 0 $\sqrt{2}$

Part 2:
Exploring the unknown

Some math problems are all about finding an unknown number. Because the number is unknown, it can't be described using digits, so mathematicians use a letter or symbol instead. Sometimes the problem can be solved by trying out different numbers in place of the symbol – such as when a coach substitutes a player in a soccer match. This is one simple example of a kind of math called **algebra**.

Even better than finding a missing number, algebra can help you find a general rule or **formula** that will explain what the answer is – not just to a single problem, but to a whole range of problems. It's also good for drawing pictures, called **graphs**, that make solutions clear and visible.

The missing number

$$(\square \times 5) \div 3 = 10 \quad \text{or} \quad (? \times 5) \div 3 = 10$$

What's the missing number?

In the questions above, the missing number is represented by the symbol $\square$ or ?.

Any symbol will do, although in algebra, you normally use a letter – often an x.

> x is often written curly, so it doesn't look like x, the symbol for multiplication.

You might write the problem above like this:

$$(5 \times x) \div 3 = 10$$

In a math test, you might be asked to figure out what x is. This means what number could you substitute for x so that the calculation still works?*

Making life easier

Doing math with letters as well as numbers might seem a little strange at first, but it's often easier than it looks. That's because much of algebra is really just about shuffling and rearranging words and numbers into much simpler, clearer statements.

> Imagine a threefold number increased by twelve, divided by the difference by which the square exceeds three.

> Ah, you mean $(3x + 12) \div (x^2 - 3)$?

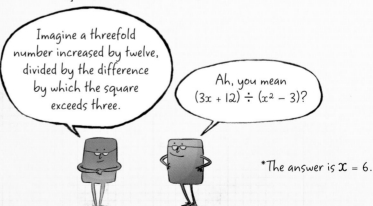

*The answer is $x = 6$.

The first symbol

One of the first mathematicians to use a symbol to represent unknown numbers was Diophantus of Alexandria in the 3rd century. Diophantus used the symbol: ς.

Celebrity number

In 1637, French mathematician René Descartes wrote a book on arithmetic, including algebra. He picked the letters x, y and z to represent unknown quantities.

The story goes that Descartes' printer had lots of spare xs, so he asked Descartes if he could use x more often than y and z.

When do you use algebra?

Although you may not realize it, you use algebra all the time in math – for instance when using any kind of **formula**, such as the formula for finding the area or volume of a shape.

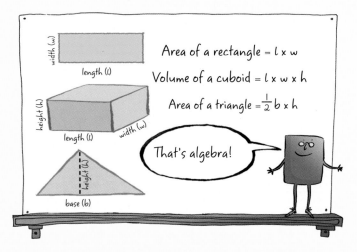

width (w)
length (l)

height (h)
length (l)   width (w)

height (h)
base (b)

Area of a rectangle = l x w

Volume of a cuboid = l x w x h

Area of a triangle = $\frac{1}{2}$ b x h

That's algebra!

Making things neat

Long sentences in algebra can take up lots of space. But there are ways to clean them up. For example:

3 x n becomes 3n

l x w x h becomes lwh

Another handy tip is to group quantities of the same letter together.

Two symbols together means they are multiplied.

3a + 4a – 2a becomes 5a

3 x a x 4 x b becomes 12ab

1,200 years ago Arab mathematician Muhammad Ibn Musa al-Khwarizmi wrote one of the first books about algebra. It was called *Hisab al-jebr wa'l -muqabala* – meaning 'calculating by restoration and balancing'.

When translated into Latin, the word *al-jebr* – meaning 'restoration' – became 'algebra'.

Algebra without x

Algebra problems don't always have an x in them. In problems about real things, other letters are often used.

For example, in a problem about a car: **s** may stand for the speed of the car, **d** for the distance it moves, and **t** for the time it takes to move.

These letters can be combined to create the formula:

$$s = \frac{d}{t}$$

It means 'speed equals distance divided by time'.

writing algebra

Statements in algebra can be broken down into smaller parts, called terms and expressions.

A **term** is made of numbers and letters multiplied together, such as 3x, 4y or 18z.

When terms are joined with + or −, this is called an **expression**, such as 3x + 4y, or 3x − 18z.

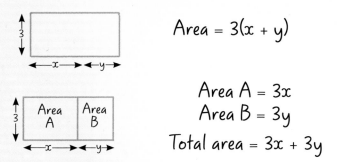

Some expressions are so neat and compressed they need unpicking, or **expanding**. Here's a compressed expression: 3(x + y). Expanded, the expression looks like this: 3x + 3y.

Either way, this expression can be used to describe the area of a rectangle that has a width of 3 and a length of x + y.

$$Area = 3(x + y)$$

$$Area\ A = 3x$$
$$Area\ B = 3y$$
$$Total\ area = 3x + 3y$$

You can susbstitute numbers for x and y to find out the area of a real rectangle. For example, if x = 5 and y = 6:

$$3(x + y)\ becomes\ 3 \times (5 + 6) = 3 \times 11$$
$$or\ (3 \times 5) + (3 \times 6) = 15 + 18$$

Either way, the answer is 33.

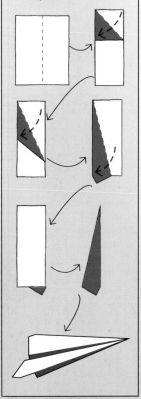

What's the point of expressions?

Creating terms and building up expressions is useful for doing long equations that don't involve numbers. Here's an example.

The Oakley family goes to a café and each person orders a drink: coffee, tea, hot chocolate, coffee, hot chocolate. One child then changes her order from hot chocolate to milk, and another from tea to milk.

The waitress writes in her notebook:

$$C + T + H + C + H - H + M - T + M$$

Each item costs a certain amount of money. But rather than writing out all the prices on the bill, the waitress simply writes:

$$2C + H + 2M$$

She has grouped all the *like terms* together. When Mrs. Oakley goes to pay, the cashier simply substitutes the correct price for each letter.

This is what algebra is about – simplifying things.

Golden rules

There are a few golden rules about how to multiply and simplify expressions. This will help you find the answers to lots of questions.

$a \times a = a^2$ 'a squared', not 'two a'

$3a \times 2 = 6a$

$a \times 2 \times b \times a = 2a^2b$

    The number goes first, then the letters

$a^2 = a \times a$

$a^3 = a \times a \times a$

$a^2 \times a^3 = a \times a \times a \times a \times a$

$= a^5$ Add the powers

x, y and z

In algebra, 'x' is often used for the first unknown in a problem. If a problem already has an x, y is used for the next unknown, then z.

> Move out of the way, you've had your turn!

Simple substitution

Lots of math problems can be solved using a formula. You may remember the formula for working out speed (see page 31):

speed = distance divided by time, or $s = \frac{d}{t}$

If you know the distance and time, you can work out the speed. Here's an example:

If James runs 100 yards in 16 seconds, how fast does he run?

Substitute 100 for **d**, and 16 for **t**, into the formula $s = \frac{d}{t}$ and you get:

$s = \frac{100}{16} = 6.25$ yards per second.

Mathe-magic

Think of a number. Double it. Add 6. Add the number you first thought of. Divide by 3. Take away the number you first thought of. What do you get?

I bet you've got 2.

Wow! How did you know?

No matter what number you start with, the answer is *always* 2. But how does this work? Algebra has the answer.
This is what happens when you follow the instructions:

x is used to stand for an unknown number. When describing any old number, mathematicians use the letter **n**.

1. **Think of a number:** n

2. **Double it:** 2n

3. **Add 6:** 2n + 6

4. **Add the first number (n):** 3n + 6

5. **Divide by 3:** (3n + 6) ÷ 3 = n + 2

6. **Take away the first number (n):** n + 2 − n
   = 2

All that's left is 2, no matter what number n is.

Equations

Doing algebra usually means turning problems into **equations**. An equation is a mathematical sentence that tells you that two expressions have the same value. For example, $5x = 3x + 6$.

To find the answer, you have to solve the equation – which means finding the missing value, x. Sometimes, it's quickest to try different numbers for x. Other times, it's easier to rearrange the equation. (You can find out how to do this, and see the answer, on page 36.)

Turning words into math

The best way to start turning a problem into an equation is to set out what you know as simple mathematical statements. For example, Arthur, Fred and Ollie buy two balloons each at a fair. Afterwards, the balloon man has eight balloons left, but how many did he start with?

You could draw a picture and count the balloons, but it might be quicker to use algebra.

Substitute x for the number of balloons the man started with. We know that:
a) each boy buys 2 balloons, making 6 balloons in total.
b) x minus 6 leaves 8 balloons.
Putting this into algebra gives: $x - 6 = 8$,

$$so \quad x = 14$$

Word problems should always have word solutions. So the final answer is:

the man started with fourteen balloons.

The oldest algebra problems in the world

Around 3,500 years ago, Ancient Egyptians showed how to solve problems about unknown quantities they called 'heaps'.

These problems have survived in a scroll known as the *Rhind Papyrus* – the oldest math book in the world. Here's one of the problems:

Rhind Papyrus: problem 24 what is the value of a **heap**, if the **heap** and a seventh of the **heap** is 19?

The answer is: $16\frac{5}{8}$

$$1\frac{1}{7} \text{ heap} = 19$$
$$\text{heap} = 19 \div 1\frac{1}{7}$$
$$= 19 \div \frac{8}{7}$$
$$= 19 \times \frac{7}{8}$$
$$= \frac{133}{8}$$

$$1 \text{ heap} = 16\frac{5}{8}$$

Rearranging the equation

Some equations are easy to solve by **rearranging** them, so that one letter is on one side of the equals sign, and everything else is on the other side.
Here's an example:

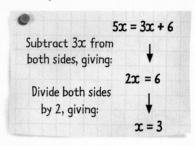

$$5x = 3x + 6$$

Subtract $3x$ from both sides, giving:

$$2x = 6$$

Divide both sides by 2, giving:

$$x = 3$$

Whenever you rearrange an equation, follow this golden rule: **whatever you do to one side of the equation, you must do to the other side.**

Seed problem

Jessie has a packet of 100 seeds, a mixture of beans, spinach and carrots. The packet says there are 20 more spinach seeds than beans, and twice as many carrot seeds as beans. But how many of each seed are there?
Here's a way to find the answer using algebra.

If the number of bean seeds = b,
the number of spinach seeds = b + 20,
and the number of carrot seeds = 2b

Adding all three makes 100 seeds, so b + b + 20 + 2b = 100
First, collect the like terms: 4b + 20 = 100
Now, rearrange the equation: 4b = 80
Rearrange again: b = 20

Use substitution to get the final answer:
There are 20 bean seeds, 40 spinach seeds, and 40 carrot seeds.

Subtract 20 from both sides. Then divide both sides by 4.

Balancing act

Algebra inventor al-Khwarizmi described algebra as calculating by 'restoration' and 'reduction'.

For al-Khwarizmi, restoration meant keeping the equation balanced by restoring or adding the same value to both sides. So A = B − C becomes A + C = B by adding C to both sides.

Reduction meant keeping the balance in an equation by reducing or subtracting the same value from both sides. So A = B + C becomes A − C = B by subtracting C from both sides.

Check your answer

If you solve an equation and want to check your answer, you can substitute it back into the original equation. For example, $2x + 6 = 16$, and you find that $x = 5$. Does this work? Well, $(2 \times 5) + 6 = 16$ is true, so the answer is correct.

Two unknowns

Some equations have more than one unknown, and can even have more than one possible set of answers.

For example, $2x + 3y = 6$.
One possible answer is: $x = 0$ and $y = 2$.
Another is $x = 3$ and $y = 0$.

Simultaneous equations

Two separate equations that share unknown values are known as **simultaneous equations**. They are called 'simultaneous' because the equations have to be solved at the same time. Here's an example.

All together now

The word simultaneous comes from the Latin *simul* which means 'at the same time' or 'together'.

He's started with his right leg – that's not simultaneous!

Bird riddle

A birdwatcher tells you what he has observed from counting the birds in two trees:
(1) If one bird flies from tree B to tree A, then tree A will have twice as many birds as tree B.
(2) If one bird flies from tree A to tree B, then both trees will have an equal number of birds.
But he doesn't tell you how many birds were in each tree at the start.

x birds

Tree A

y birds

Tree B

You could figure this out by creating two equations:
Let tree A have x birds, and tree B have y birds.

(1) tells us that $x + 1 = 2(y - 1)$
Remove the parenthses to get $x + 1 = 2y - 2$
Simplify to get $x = 2y - 3$

(2) tells us that $x - 1 = y + 1$
Simplify to get $x = y + 2$

Combining these equations, you get the value of y and then x.
$$x = 2y - 3 \text{ and } x = y + 2,$$
$$\text{so } 2y - 3 = y + 2$$
$$y - 3 = 2$$
$$y = 5$$
No we can substitute y = 5 into the equation $x = y + 2$:
$$x = 5 + 2 = 7$$

Tree A Final answer: tree A started with 7 birds; tree B started with 5 birds. Tree B

Drawing equations

Another way of looking at equations is to draw a picture of them, called a graph. Some equations form straight lines, others form curves.

Unchanging lines

When an equation simply has x or y as a fixed number, it produces a vertical or horizontal straight line. For example, look at these two graphs:

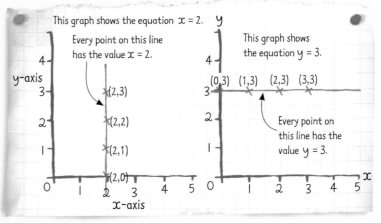

This graph shows the equation $x = 2$.

Every point on this line has the value $x = 2$.

(2,3)
(2,2)
(2,1)
(2,0)

y-axis

x-axis

This graph shows the equation $y = 3$.

(0,3) (1,3) (2,3) (3,3)

Every point on this line has the value $y = 3$.

Fly on the ceiling

Graphs are based on an idea invented by the French mathematician René Descartes. The story goes that while Descartes was in bed one day, he noticed a fly crawling across the ceiling.

Descartes thought about how to describe the exact position of the fly to another person. He came up with the idea of giving its distance from fixed horizontal and vertical lines.

He called the horizontal line the x-axis and the vertical line the y-axis. That's why graphs have an x axis and a y-axis.

Linear equations

An equation that gives a simple link between x and y makes a straight, but sloping line. For example $y = 2x + 1$.

To draw this on a graph, start by making a table, substituting different numbers for x to work out the corresponding y value.

This is substitution: choose a value for x, solve the calculation, and find out what y is.

Table of solutions to the equation: $y = 2x + 1$.

x	-2	-1	0	1	2
$y = 2x + 1$	-3	-1	1	3	5

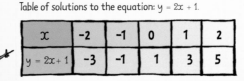

Try a few negative numbers, too.

Next, draw an x-axis and a y-axis and number them. Use each pair of values in the table as coordinates, and mark them as crosses. Then, draw a line that runs through all the crosses.

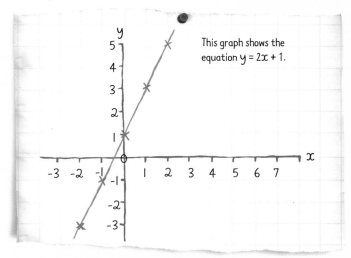

This graph shows the equation $y = 2x + 1$.

Any old line

Any straight line can be written as an equation using letters like this: $y = mx + b$

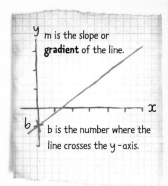

m is the slope or **gradient** of the line.

b is the number where the line crosses the y-axis.

A simple curve

Equations that contain an x^2 make a curve. For example, here's what happens if you plot the graph of the equation $y = x^2 + x - 2$.

Table of solutions for:
$y = x^2 + x - 2$

x	-2	-1	0	1	2
$y = x^2 + x - 2$	0	-2	-2	0	4

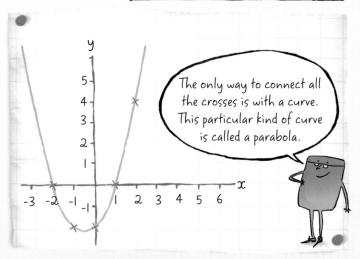

The only way to connect all the crosses is with a curve. This particular kind of curve is called a parabola.

Area equations

Any equation that includes x^2, and no higher power of x, is called a **quadratic equation.** Some of the first people to describe them were tax collectors in Ancient Babylon. They used them to calculate a certain proportion of the total area of a field, so they could charge farmers the right amount of tax.

Real curves

Scientists often use equations and graphs to model real things such as the flight path of a rocket or the shape made by a beam of light.

Beams of light

The equation:
$x^2 - y^2 = -1$ makes a broken pair of curves called a hyperbola. This kind of graph models the shape made by light shining from an overhead lamp.

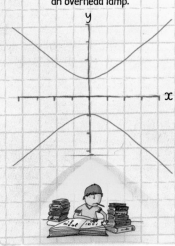

Rocket route

The equation:
$h = -t^2 + 10t + 16$ makes a parabola. This kind of equation models the path of a rocket, where h describes how high the rocket is, and t shows how much time has passed since the rocket launched.

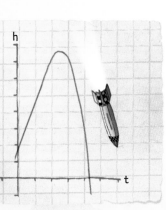

Moving in a circle

The equation $x^2 + y^2 = 4$ makes a circle.

It could be used to program a machine to make a specific size of bicycle wheel.

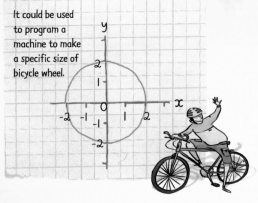

Waves of sound

Sound travels through the air in a wave of pressure known as a sine wave. Here's an equation to draw a sine wave: $y = A\sin(kx)$. A describes how loud the sound is, and k describes its pitch.

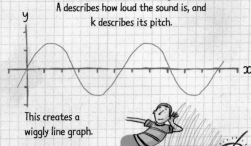

This creates a wiggly line graph.

Spirals

17th-century mathematician Jakob Bernoulli uncovered a complex equation that created a spiral matching the pattern on a snail shell: $r = ae^{b\theta}$.

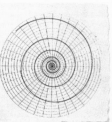

Finding the answer with a graph

You can use graphs to solve simultaneous equations. If you plot two simultaneous equations on the same graph, the point where they meet gives the solution.

Tommy tells Iona that two cakes need six eggs in total and one cake needs two more eggs than the other. How many eggs does each cake need?

Let's say x represents the number of eggs for one cake, and y represents the number of eggs for the other. The two cakes together need 6 eggs, so $x + y = 6$. And one cake needs two more eggs, so $y = x + 2$.

1) $x + y = 6$
2) $y = x + 2$

This is a pair of simultaneous equations.

Plotted on a graph you get:

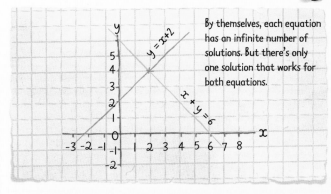

By themselves, each equation has an infinite number of solutions. But there's only one solution that works for both equations.

The two lines meet when $x = 2$ and $y = 4$. So Iona needs two eggs for one cake and four for the other.

Using graphs

Graphs can be useful for all sorts of things, from converting measurements to showing the speed of a journey, or even studying how well groceries in a supermarket sell. Find out more in Part 4 of this book.

School journey

Chloé catches a bus to get to school. This graph shows a typical journey for Chloé.

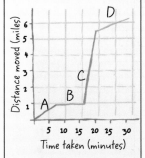

A Walking
B Waiting for bus
C On bus
D Walking

The slope of the line, or **gradient**, represents the speed Chloé is moving at each stage.

Where the line is horizontal, she is standing still.

Where the gradient is greatest, her journey was quickest – in this case, while she was on the bus.

Seeing patterns

Drawing a sequence

The numbers 1, 3, 6, 10 are the start of a sequence called **triangular numbers.** You can see why they're called triangular if you draw them out using dots, like this:

1 •   3 •
              • •

6 •   10 •
   • •   • •
  • • •   • • •
              • • • •

To build the next triangle, you have to add another row of dots. The bottom row always has one more dot than the row above.

The first triangular number is 1

The second is 1 + 2 = 3

The third is 1 + 2 + 3 = 6

The fourth is 1 + 2 + 3 + 4 = 10

To find the fifth triangular number, you could start with the fourth triangular number, then add 5. This is the same as adding up all the numbers from 1 to 5.

1 + 2 + 3 + 4 + 5 = 15, the 5th triangular number.

To find the 50th triangular number, add all the numbers from 1 to 50 – or turn to page 45 to find a quicker way...

Algebra is an excellent tool for describing patterns and relationships. A list of numbers that follows a pattern is called a **sequence**.

> Each number in a sequence is called a **term**.

Some patterns are easier to spot than others. Take a look at this sequence:

$$2 \quad 7 \quad 12 \quad 17 \quad 22 \quad 27 \quad 32...$$

The pattern is that each time 5 is added to get the next number. Here's a trickier sequence:

$$3 \quad 6 \quad 11 \quad 18 \quad 27 \quad 38 \quad 51...$$

One way to find the pattern here is to look at which numbers are being added *between* the terms. In this example, each term is created by adding the next biggest odd number.

$$\overset{+3}{3} \quad \overset{+5}{6} \quad \overset{+7}{11} \quad \overset{+9}{18} \quad \overset{+11}{27} \quad \overset{+13}{38} \quad 51...$$

Sequences don't have to be about numbers. Can you see what shape comes next in this sequence?*

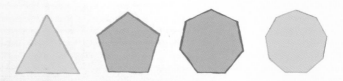

*The answer is on page 93.

Finding a rule

Take a look at this sequence:

1 4 7 10 13 16 19...

Hint: try comparing this sequence to the three times table...

This sequence starts at 1 and adds 3 each time. The next number in the sequence will be 19 + 3 = 22. But how do you work out the next term, or the 24th term, or any particular term − called the nth term, where n represents any position in the sequence?

A quick way to answer this is to find an expression, or **rule**, that describes the sequence. The pattern in this sequence is the three times table minus 2.

The rule for this sequence is: the nth term = $3n − 2$. To find, say, the 24th term, substitute 24 for n. This gives: $(3 \times 24) − 2$
$= 72 − 2 = 70.$

Drawing sequences

You can plot the terms of a sequence on a graph.

If the difference between each term is the same amount, the points will lie on a straight line:

Graph of sequence $t = 3n − 2$

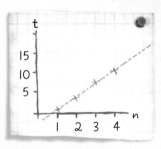

Square number sequences

Some sequences have more complex rules. For example:

$$1 \overset{+3}{\frown} 4 \overset{+5}{\frown} 9 \overset{+7}{\frown} 16 \overset{+9}{\frown} 25...$$

The *difference* between each term increases by 2 each time. So the next number in the sequence will be:
$$25 + (9 + 2) = 36.$$
To find the rule, you need to compare each term with its corresponding position in the sequence.

If the difference between the terms increases each time, the points will lie on a curve that gets steeper and steeper:

Graph of sequence $t = n^2$

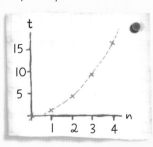

Position	1st	2nd	3rd	4th	...n^{th}
Term	1	4	9	16	...n^2

Each term is the square of its position in the sequence.

The rule for this sequence is: the nth term = n^2

43

Fantastic Fibonacci

One famous sequence is named after Italian mathematician Leonardo Fibonacci, who wrote it down about 800 years ago. The first two terms are 1 and 1. Then the rule is: create the next term by adding the two previous terms together. So, the numbers grow rapidly.

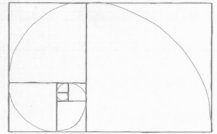

An easier way to add

Fibonacci was the first person in Europe to write a math book using Hindu-Arabic numerals. He found them much easier to use than Roman numerals.

His *Book of Calculation*, published in 1202, persuaded other mathematicians in Europe to try them. These numerals are what people use today.

Fibonacci squares

The Fibonacci sequence describes certain shapes, too. Look at this set of squares:

> The two smallest squares have sides of length 1.

> Each further square is made by adding the side lengths of the previous two squares.

8

13

5

2

1 1

3

Fibonacci everywhere

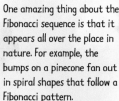

One amazing thing about the Fibonacci sequence is that it appears all over the place in nature. For example, the bumps on a pinecone fan out in spiral shapes that follow a Fibonacci pattern.

The pinecone has 8 spirals going one way (marked in yellow) and 13 the other (marked in blue). 8 and 13 are consecutive numbers in the Fibonacci sequence.

A curious thing happens if you draw a curved line through each square: you create a spiral.

Many creatures, such as snails, grow shells in stages that follow the same pattern as the Fibonacci sequence, and so end up in a spiral.

Astonishing algebra

Carl Gauss was one of the greatest mathematicians of the 18th and 19th centuries. When he was only ten years old, he is said to have astounded his teacher and class by coming up with a brilliant solution to a math problem.

The teacher set the class the task of adding up all the numbers from one to a hundred. He thought this would take them at least half an hour.

But within minutes, Gauss had the answer.

5,050.

Here's how he did it:

1. First, he looked at triangular numbers.

1   3   6   10

10 is the number of dots in a triangle with sides of 4 dots. It's also the answer to the sum 1 + 2 + 3 + 4.

2. Gauss saw that if you have a triangle with sides of 4, you can put two identical triangles together to make a rectangle with sides measuring 4 dots wide and 4 + 1 dots long.

3. The number of dots in the rectangle is
$4 \times (4 + 1)$.
The number of dots in each triangle is
$1 + 2 + 3 + 4$
There are two triangles in the rectangle,
so $2 \times (1 + 2 + 3 + 4) = 4 \times (4 + 1)$.
Or, rearranging the equation,
$(1 + 2 + 3 + 4) = \dfrac{4 \times (4+1)}{2}$

4. Gauss then turned this into a rule for adding up all the numbers to the nth term:
$1 + 2 + 3 + \dots + n = \dfrac{n \times (n+1)}{2}$

5. To solve the teacher's problem, he substituted 100 for n:
So $1 + 2 + \dots + 100 = \dfrac{100 \times 101}{2} = 5,050$

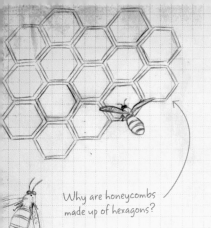

Why are honeycombs made up of hexagons?

What's a fractal?

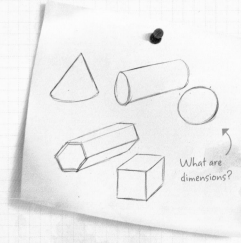

What are dimensions?

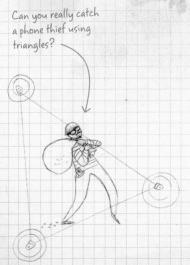

Can you really catch a phone thief using triangles?

How did an Ancient Greek scholar measure an Egyptian pyramid without climbing it?

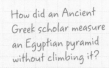

Part 3:
Shape, space and measurement

Examining the size and shape of things is very important in everyday life. For example, if a truck driver knows how tall and wide the truck is, she'll know whether it will fit under a low bridge.

Most objects, from a sleek sports car to an enormous blue whale, have uneven, **irregular** shapes – making them tricky to measure accurately. But even irregularly shaped objects can be broken down into **regular** shapes, which can be analyzed following mathematical rules.

Geometry

The mathematics of shapes is called **geometry**, which means 'world measure' in Greek. Ancient Greeks gave it this name because they used math based on shapes to help answer questions such as 'how big is the Earth?'

Find out how one man calculated the circumference of the Earth, on page 63.

Euclid's Elements

Ancient Greek scholar Euclid is known as the father of geometry.

He wrote a famous study of geometry, *Elements*, around 2,300 years ago. In it, he examined circles, triangles, cones and pyramids, as well as ratios and proportions. It was used as a textbook for over 2,000 years.

Shape up

All objects have size and shape – whether they're as large as planets or as tiny as atoms, regular like boxes or irregular like hands.

Everything takes up space, too. You can use words to define shape, and numbers and measurements to describe an object's size, and how much space it takes up.

Flat shapes

A flat drawing of a shape is called two-dimensional, or 2-D, because it has two **dimensions**: length and width.

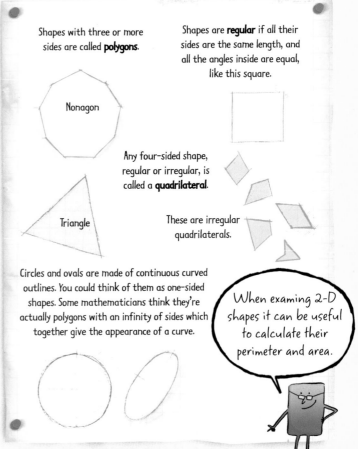

Shapes with three or more sides are called **polygons**.

Shapes are **regular** if all their sides are the same length, and all the angles inside are equal, like this square.

Nonagon

Any four-sided shape, regular or irregular, is called a **quadrilateral**.

Triangle

These are irregular quadrilaterals.

Circles and ovals are made of continuous curved outlines. You could think of them as one-sided shapes. Some mathematicians think they're actually polygons with an infinity of sides which together give the appearance of a curve.

When examing 2-D shapes it can be useful to calculate their perimeter and area.

Solid shapes

Solid shapes, such as balls or boxes, are described as three-dimensional, or 3-D. They have length and width like 2-D shapes, but they also have a third dimension – depth. Here are some common examples:

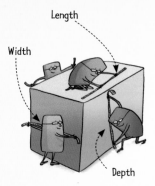

Length

Width

Depth

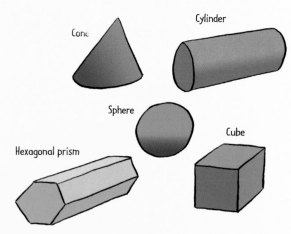

Cone

Cylinder

Sphere

Cube

Hexagonal prism

Real objects

Truly 2-D objects are very rare in the real world, as most things have thickness. But 3-D shapes are everywhere...

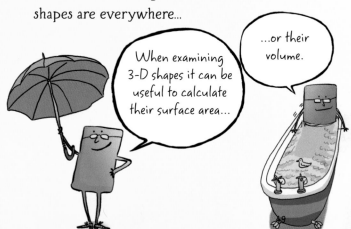

When examining 3-D shapes it can be useful to calculate their surface area...

...or their volume.

Extra dimensions

This line has just one dimension, usually written as x.

_____ x

This square has two dimensions, usually written as x and y.

y

x

This cube has three dimensions: x, y and z.

z y x

Although our universe is 3-D, some people have tried to imagine what it would be like to have more dimensions.

In the late 19th century, British mathematician Charles Hinton imagined adding a fourth dimension to a cube, creating a shape he called a tesseract.

It's very hard to visualize a 4-D object in a 3-D world. This computer drawing of a tesseract, also known as a hypercube, pictures it as a cube trapped within a cube.

Measuring shapes

Being able to measure flat and solid shapes, to find out their
dimensions, mass and volume, can be incredibly useful.
Imagine you're building a new sports complex...

How much paint will you
need for the walls? You
need to work out the area.
Area of a rectangle = l w

How many bricks will you need
to build the outer walls? You
need to work out the area of
each wall. If it's a curved wall,
it might be easier to break it
up into smaller sections.

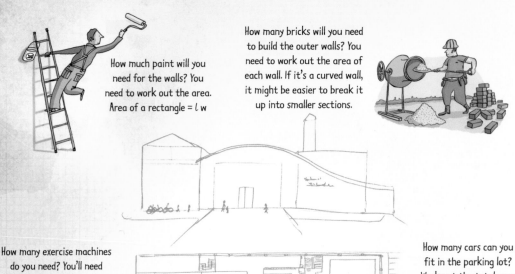

How many exercise machines
do you need? You'll need
to research which types
of machines will be most
popular, and measure how
many of them will fit into
the gym.

How many cars can you
fit in the parking lot?
Work out the total area
of your parking lot, then
divide by the amount of
space needed for each car,
including space for access.

How much water will you need
to fill the pool? Work out the
volume, or the amount of
space, inside the pool.
Volume = l w d

Once you know the volume of
water, use a ratio to work
out how much chlorine you
need to add to it.

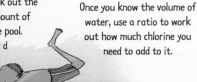

Useful units

Different things are measured using different **units** – for example, length can be measured in feet (ft) and miles and mass in pounds (lbs) and ounces (oz). Each unit belongs to a certain type of measurement, so when you see it you know what's being measured.

This plank is 1 foot by 5 feet.

And it's 10 pounds.

Big and small

You can describe the same measurement in different ways. A car that has a mass of 1 ton can also be said to have a mass of 2,000 pounds, or 32,000 ounces. These numbers all describe the same mass, although the last two are so unwieldy you probably wouldn't use them. Different orders of magnitude (see page 24) suit different units. Some things are so very big or small that special units have been invented to describe them.

Light moves so quickly that in one year, it will travel over 9×10^{15} meters, or 9 petameters.

Atoms are incredibly small. The smallest atoms each measure just 62×10^{-12} m across. It's easier to say they are 62 picometers wide.

A byte is a unit of computer memory. A new laptop might have 4 terabytes of memory – that's 4×10^{12} bytes.

Mixed measures

The US customary measurement system uses units such as ounces, pounds and tons, and feet, yards and miles.

The metric system dates from 1799. It uses units such as g, kg, cm and m.

Although the metric system is not used in everyday measurements in the US, it's often used in the armed forces, science, aviation and government.

There are 16 ounces in a pound, 2,000 pounds in a ton, and 12 inches in a foot.

Unique unit

A smoot is a unit of length named after Oliver R. Smoot. '1 smoot' is the length of Oliver's body, which his university friends used to measure the length of Harvard Bridge in Boston. The bridge was measured as 364.4 smoots long, which is actually 678.1 yards.

= 1 smoot

Coincidentally, Smoot later became head of the American National Standards Institute, which makes decisions on units and measurement.

Fair guess

Fairs and carnivals often hold competitions based on estimating measurements. For example, how many candies are in this jar? Here's a tip: count the candies on the bottom layer. Then count the number of layers. Multiplying these numbers will get you pretty close to the real answer, so long as there aren't any huge jawbreakers hiding in the middle.

Counting flocks

Birdwatchers often like to count the number of birds in a flock. This isn't easy, especially if the birds keep moving. The best way is to first count a small group of birds in an imaginary block. Then estimate how many times this block shape fits into the whole flock.

To get a more accurate result, you could do the same thing two or three times, and work out the average.

Estimating measurements

Knowing simple math about shapes can help you make quick calculations about crowds. For example, imagine you see a squadron of alien invaders pouring out of a spaceship, and you want to work out how many alien soldiers there are...

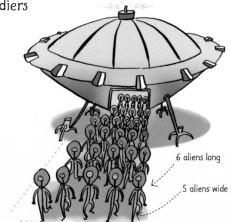

If the aliens are standing in a roughly rectangular-shaped group, you could calculate the area of the rectangle.

Area = width x length

5 aliens wide and 6 aliens deep gives an estimated total of 30. There are actually 2 extra, smaller aliens squished in there so the real total is 32.

6 aliens long

5 aliens wide

Real world estimates

If you know how long it takes to walk a typical journey, say from your house to a friend's house, you can use this to estimate how long another walk would take.

Don't forget that in real life no two walks are the same, so you'll need to account for extra variables in your estimate. For example, another journey might go up a steep hill, or you might feel tired that day. But an estimate can still be a useful rough guide.

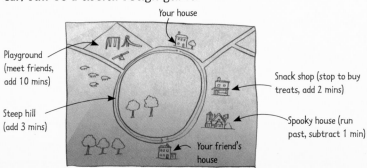

Your house

Playground (meet friends, add 10 mins)

Snack shop (stop to buy treats, add 2 mins)

Steep hill (add 3 mins)

Spooky house (run past, subtract 1 min)

Your friend's house

52   Blue and red route both = 1 mile

Time to walk blue route = 23 mins

Time to walk red route = 11 mins

Packing up puzzle

Packing shapes neatly into a box is a kind of math problem. Hundreds of years ago, people in China turned this sort of shape problem into a puzzle known as a tangram. Here's an example:

Tangrams are a combination of seven shapes, called tans, cut out of a square:

Can you see how to use the seven tans to make one big triangle?

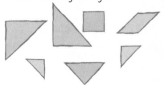

(The answer is on page 93.)

Kitchen guesses

Recipes often list precise amounts of each ingredient, sometimes in units of weight. But experienced cooks know how much space a particular weight of flour or butter normally takes up, so they can estimate the quantity without using a set of scales.

Paint problem

If a can of paint will cover an area of 60yds², how many cans will you need to paint this room? You don't need to paint the floor, ceiling, door or window.

Wall A = 10yds x 3yds = 30yds²
Wall B = 15yds x 3yds = 45yds²
Wall C = 10yds x 3yds = 30yds²
Wall D = 15yds x 3yds = 45yds²
Door = 1yd x 2yds = 2yds²
Window = 2yds x 2yds = 4yds²

Sketch of room to paint

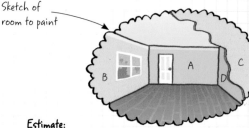

Exact calculation:

Walls A + C = 2(10yds x 3yds) = 60yds²
Walls B + D = 2(15yds x 3yds) = 90yds²
Total wall area = 150yds²
150yds² − (door + window)
150yds² − (2yds² + 4yds²) = 144yds²
144yds² ÷ 60yds² = 2.4

You need 2.4 cans, so you'll need to buy 3 cans of paint. (And you should have 0.6 of a can left over to fix any mistakes.)

Estimate:

Alternatively, for a rough estimate, you could work out the area of the biggest wall and multiply by 4.

4 x (3yds x 15yds) = 180yds²
180 − (door + window)
180 − (2yds² + 4yds²) = 174yds²
174yds² ÷ 60yds² = 2.9

This method suggests you'll need about 2.9 cans, so you'll need to buy 3 cans of paint – which is correct.

Going in circles

Circles are everywhere.

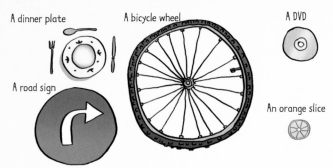

A dinner plate   A bicycle wheel   A DVD

A road sign

An orange slice

Because circles are so common, mathematicians have spent thousands of years studying them. They've cut them up and named different lines and slices.

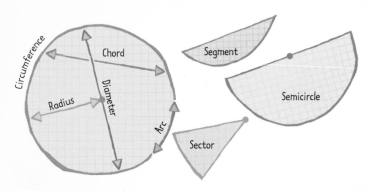

Circumference

Chord   Segment

Radius   Diameter

Semicircle

Arc

Sector

π or τ?

π represents the number that defines the relationship between a circle's circumference and its *diameter*. A number called tau (τ) defines the link between circumference and *radius*. τ is 2 x π, or about 6.28.

τ can be more useful than π. For example the circumference of a circle is defined by the formula 2x π x radius, but it's quicker to say circumference = τ x radius.

No matter how big or how small a circle is, if you divide its circumference by its diameter you always get the same number. It's known as pi — or by the symbol π — a name given to it by the Ancient Greeks. It's an irrational number, usually rounded off to 3.14.

In 2011, a supercomputer in Tokyo calculated π to a billion decimal places.

Celebrity number: π

π turns up in lots of mathematical definitions about circles.

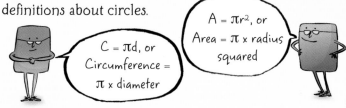

$C = \pi d$, or Circumference = π x diameter

$A = \pi r^2$, or Area = π x radius squared

Ancient Greek mathematician Archimedes used π to work out properties of cylinders and spheres:

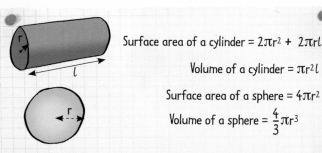

Surface area of a cylinder = $2\pi r^2 + 2\pi r l$

Volume of a cylinder = $\pi r^2 l$

Surface area of a sphere = $4\pi r^2$

Volume of a sphere = $\frac{4}{3}\pi r^3$

But beware, π is irrational and can't be written as an exact number, so any math done using π is only ever an approximation.

Turning around

Circles help describe turns, or **angles**, inside shapes. The amount of turn is measured in degrees. Turning around in a full circle is defined as 360 degrees or 360°.

A quarter turn is 90°.

You can describe a turn or angle as a fraction of a full circle. Some angles have particular names:

A half turn is 180°.

Less than 90 degrees: an acute angle

More than 90 degrees, less than 180 degrees: an obtuse angle

More than 180 degrees: a reflex angle

Exactly 90 degrees: a right angle

Archimedes and π

For a long time π was known as Archimedes' constant, named after Ancient Greek genius Archimedes. He figured out an accurate way to estimate the value of π over 2,200 years ago.

He drew two 96-sided polygons, one just outside a circle...

...and one just inside.

He calculated the area of both polygons, and used these to estimate the area of the circle. Then he figured out π using the formula $\pi = \frac{A}{r^2}$.

Archimedes calculated π as 3.14185. Modern calculators round it off to 3.141592653 – so he wasn't far off.

55

Tricks with triangles

Triangles are three-sided shapes and get their name from the fact that they contain three angles. The branch of mathematics that deals with angles and triangles is called **trigonometry**. It's also used to study shapes with curves, such as circles and waves.

Triangle basics

There are four main types of triangles: equilateral, isosceles, scalene and right triangles. Whatever the type of triangle, its angles always add up to 180°.

   Triangles can form different kinds of 3-D solids, including triangle-based pyramids, square-based pyramids and triangular prisms.

Thales and pyramids

Thales was a Ancient Greek philosopher who lived about 2,600 years ago. He wanted to know how high a pyramid was, but it was too tall to measure easily.

He saw that at a certain time of day, the length of his shadow equalled his own height. So, to calculate the pyramid's height, he measured its shadow at that same time of day.

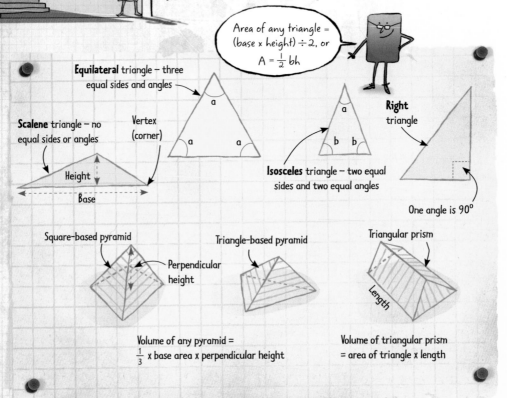

Area of any triangle = (base x height) ÷ 2, or $A = \frac{1}{2} bh$

Equilateral triangle – three equal sides and angles

Scalene triangle – no equal sides or angles

Vertex (corner)

Height

Base

Isosceles triangle – two equal sides and two equal angles

Right triangle

One angle is 90°

Square-based pyramid

Perpendicular height

Triangle-based pyramid

Triangular prism

Length

Volume of any pyramid = $\frac{1}{3}$ x base area x perpendicular height

Volume of triangular prism = area of triangle x length

Constructing a triangle

It's easy to draw a triangle if you know how long all three sides are. But you can also construct a triangle if you know the length of two sides and the angle between them:

1. Draw one of the known sides.

2. Use a protractor to mark the known angle at one end.

3. Draw the other known side in the direction of this angle.

4. Connect both lines to form the final side.

Or if you know one side and two angles:

1. Draw the known side.

2. Use a protractor to mark the known angles at each end.

3. Draw long lines in the direction of both angles.

4. The lines will cross at the final corner of the triangle.

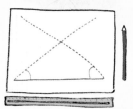

Map a location with triangulation

Surveyors calculate the lengths and angles of triangles to draw more accurate maps – a process known as **triangulation**. Here's how it works:

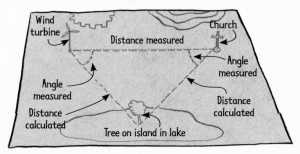

Wind turbine

Church

Distance measured

Angle measured

Angle measured

Distance calculated

Distance calculated

Tree on island in lake

The surveyors choose three landmarks. After measuring one distance and two angles, they can plot a triangle and calculate the remaining distances. Then they pick a new landmark, and create a new triangle in the same way – until they've mapped out a whole area.

Triangle theorem

One of the most famous triangle facts is about right triangles. It shows how the lengths of the three sides are related:

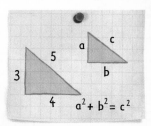

5
3
4

a
c
b

$$a^2 + b^2 = c^2$$

In Europe and the USA, the theorem is named after Ancient Greek mathematician Pythagoras. He proved it about 2,500 years ago. In China, it's named after mathematician Shang Gao, who came up with it independently about 2,200 years ago.

Catching crooks

Police officers sometimes locate a criminals by triangulating signals from their cell phones. First, the phone company traces the phone's unique signal. Then, they find out which three phone towers are closest to that signal.

The strength of the signal between each tower and the phone can pinpoint the phone's exact location.

Representing shapes

Knowing how to draw shapes accurately allows architects, artists and computer programmers to create images of 3-D things – from cars to palaces to alien worlds.

Coordinates in 3-D

To plot a 3-D shape on a grid you need to use 3 axes: x, y and z. And to locate each point on the shape, you will need an x, y and z coordinate.

This point is (4, 3, 3.)

A designer has used computer-generated shapes to build up a basic image of a car. This makes it easy to make design changes and see how they might look.

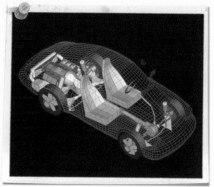

When architects design a building, they begin by drawing a plan and elevations. A **plan** shows the view of the building from above. An **elevation** shows what it looks like from the front or the side.

Plan

Side elevation

Front elevation

Super scale

To make a drawing of something big fit onto a sheet of paper, you need to reduce all the dimensions by the same amount. This is called **drawing to scale**.

This is important for creating accurate maps. Maps have little keys that explain the scale using ratios, so you can figure out what a distance on the map would be in real life.

An actual building, or a 3-D model, looks very different from its plan and elevations. This is because you see different parts of it from different points of view.

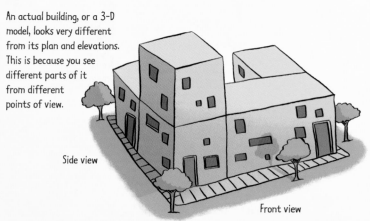

Side view

Front view

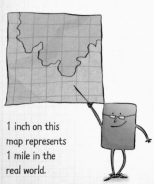

1 inch on this map represents 1 mile in the real world.

Netting shapes

If you cut along some of the edges of a 3-D shape, such as a box, and unfold it out flat, you'd make something called a **net**. See if you can match these nets to the 3-D shapes below:*

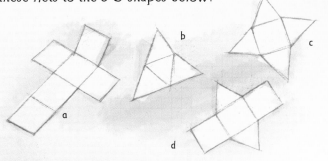
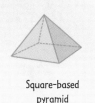

a

b

c

d

Square-based pyramid

Cube

Triangle-based pyramid

Triangular prism

Model math

A 3-D representation of an object is called a **model**. It might be the engine of a plane, a building, a sculpture or even a scene in a virtual reality game.

Designers of computer games use mathematical programs to analyze elevations, plans and nets from illustrations or photographs. This information is then used to recreate objects as images on screen.

Mathematical models can be perfect, but they can only ever approximate things in the real world. For example, a model of a brick wall might be perfectly smooth, but no brick wall is perfectly smooth in reality. This is why some virtual reality images look very fake.

Celebrity number

Ancient scholars thought the most pleasing rectangle was one that had a special ratio between its long and short sides.

They called it the **golden ratio**, and it was represented by the Greek letter ϕ, called phi.

The ratio was popular with artists and architects. Like π, ϕ is an irrational number. Its value is approximately 1.618.

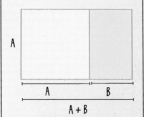

A

A

B

A + B

The ratio of A:B is the same as the ratio of A+B: A.

The golden ratio was used to build sections of the Mosque of Uqba in North Africa, such as the minaret shown here.

Playing with shapes

When a shape's appearance is altered, it is said to have been been transformed.
Mathematical **transformations** include rotating, translating, enlarging and reflecting.

Rotating means turning a shape around a point, such as one of its corners.

B is a rotation of A.

A   B

The shape stays
the same size.

Translating a shape means moving it up, down, left or right. Its size and angle stay the same.

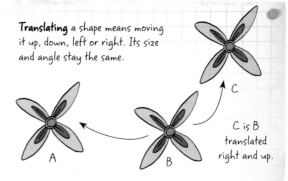

C

C is B
translated
right and up.

A   B

A is B translated
left and up.

Scaling something means changing its size in relation to a fixed point. The length of all the sides increases by the same factor, but the angles stay the same.

The factor of increase is called the **scale factor**. A scale factor of 2 means the sides will double in size.

The blue butterfly is an enlargement of the red butterfly by a scale factor of 2.

It's possible to 'enlarge' a shape by a fractional factor. This means it will shrink down in size.

The red butterfly is a fractional enlargement of the blue butterfly. Its sides are $\frac{1}{2}$ the size of the blue butterfly.

Reflecting is a transformation that happens when a shape is flipped across a line. It's like looking in a mirror.

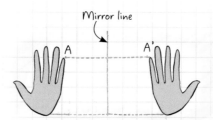

Mirror line

A   A'

The reflection of point A is called point A'. The shape and its reflection are the same distance from the mirror line.

Shapes are said to be **congruent** if they have the same size and shape.

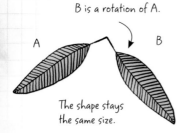

Symmetry

Some shapes have mirror lines inside themselves. These shapes are described as **symmetrical**. The mirror line is called a line of symmetry. If you cut out a shape and then try to fold it so that it makes two perfectly overlapping halves, unfold it and then see how many ways you can do this, you'll find all its lines of symmetry.

This triangle has 3 lines of symmetry. It can be folded in half three different ways.

The triangle also has rotational symmetry of order 3.

Some shapes can be turned all the way around and fit exactly onto themselves. This is called **rotational symmetry**.

This z has rotational symmetry of order 2. When turned 360°, it looks exactly like itself two times on the rotation, once at 180° and again at 360°.

Finding fractals

One branch of geometry involves finding equations that can be drawn on a graph to make a shape. In the 19th century, German mathematician Karl Weierstrass came up with an algorithm that drew a very unusual kind of shape – a shape that went on forever, repeating itself on a smaller and smaller scale.

In the 1960s, French mathematician Benoît Mandelbrot studied these patterns and came up with a name for them: **fractals**. Fractals are shapes that exhibit something called self-similarity – the same pattern is repeated at different scales, so you see it again and again as you zoom in on the shape.

Natural fractals

If you look closely at some objects, part of their shape repeats itself over and over again. These are called fractal objects.

Fractals were observed in nature centuries ago by Italian mathematician Fibonacci, although he didn't name them. They can be seen in snowflakes, flowers and even clouds.

A snowflake seen under a microscope

Here's one of Mandelbrot's fractals, drawn using a computer.

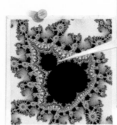

No matter how closely you zoom in, the same pattern is always visible.

Tessellations

A **tessellation** is a repeating, symmetrical pattern of shapes with no overlaps or gaps. The shapes don't have to be identical – for example, the surface of a ball can be made by tessellating hexagons and pentagons.

2-D tessellations are often used to make tiles to decorate floors or walls. Tessellations exist in 3-D, too, for example, in the dense structure of a honeycomb.

Regular tessellations

Only three regular shapes can tessellate: equilateral triangles, squares and hexagons.

Tessellations in art

Hundreds of years ago, Islamic artists used various shapes (including stars, triangles and crescents) to design tessellating tiles. They used them to decorate palaces.

A section of wall from the Alhambra Palace in Granada, Spain

In the early 20th century, Dutch artist M. C. Escher was inspired by the Alhambra to create his own tessellations. He often designed shapes to look like interlocking animals.

An Escher pattern made up of birds and fish

Do-it-yourself: tessellating pattern

Here's a simple example of how to play around with a simple tessellating shape to make a more complex, but still tessellating, pattern:

1. First, draw out a square.

2. Cut a section from one side of the square. It doesn't matter what shape you cut out.

3. Add that section to the other side of the square. You can draw a picture to fill the new shape if you like.

This shape tessellates, too.

4. Copy the shape again and again to build up your tessellation.

Measuring the Earth

Understanding how shapes work can be
very useful, as Ancient Greek mathematician Eratosthenes
discovered. He used his knowledge of circles, triangles and
angles to estimate the circumference of the Earth around
2,200 years ago. Here's how he did it.

ERATOSTHENES LIVED IN ALEXANDRIA IN NORTHERN EGYPT.

AS PART OF HIS STUDIES OF ASTRONOMY, HE MEASURED SHADOWS CAST BY THE SUN.

AT NOON PRECISELY ON MIDSUMMER'S DAY, THE SUN CAST NO SHADOW ONTO A SUNDIAL IN SYENE, A TOWN IN SOUTHERN EGYPT.

BUT AT EXACTLY THE SAME TIME IN ALEXANDRIA, THE SUN CAST A SLIM SHADOW ONTO A SUNDIAL.

I estimate this angle as just over 7°.

AT THE TIME, DISTANCES WERE MEASURED IN UNITS CALLED STADIA. THE DISTANCE FROM ALEXANDRIA TO SYENE WAS ABOUT 5,040 STADIA.

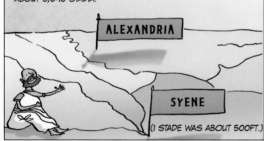

ALEXANDRIA

SYENE

(1 STADE WAS ABOUT 500FT.)

SINCE THE SURFACE OF THE EARTH IS ROUGHLY CIRCULAR, HE CONCLUDED THAT THE ARC BETWEEN THE TOWNS WAS 7° OUT OF A TOTAL OF 360°, OR APPROXIMATELY $\frac{1}{50}$. SO THE DISTANCE BETWEEN THE TOWNS MUST BE $\frac{1}{50}$ OF THE TOTAL CIRCUMFERENCE OF THE EARTH.

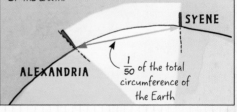

SYENE

ALEXANDRIA

$\frac{1}{50}$ of the total circumference of the Earth

SO, HOW BIG IS THE EARTH?

IF $\frac{1}{50}$ OF THE EARTH'S CIRCUMFERENCE IS 5,040 STADIA, THEN THE WHOLE CIRCUMFERENCE IS 5,040 × 50.

THIS GIVES A TOTAL OF 252,000 STADIA, WHICH IS THE EQUIVALENT OF 23,490 MILES.

MODERN MEASUREMENTS GIVE THE CIRCUMFERENCE OF THE EARTH AS 24,900 MILES, SO ERATOSTHENES' ESTIMATE WASN'T FAR OFF.

HE WAS A LITTLE OFF BECAUSE ALEXANDRIA IS NOT DUE NORTH OF SYENE, AND THE EARTH ISN'T ACTUALLY A PERFECT SPHERE – IT'S A LITTLE FLAT AT THE NORTH AND SOUTH POLES.

What does average mean?

Avg. contents: 23 seeds

What are pie charts for?

Why do people conduct surveys?

Can math be unfair?

Part 4:
Facts and figures

Deaths from
hospital infections

Deaths from
wounds in battle

Deaths from
other causes

During the 1850s, war raged in eastern Europe, and
thousands of wounded soldiers were sent to makeshift
hospitals. One of the nurses working at such a hospital was
named Florence Nightingale. She's remembered today for
greatly improving hospital conditions. But the secret to her
success was math – specifically **statistics**.

Statistics is all about collecting and analyzing information.
Nightingale found that many more soldiers died in hospitals
than on the battlefield, often because of poor hygiene. She
turned these figures into a chart and used it to persuade
politicians and generals to clean up hospitals.

Read on to find out more about how well-researched,
well-presented statistics can be a powerful tool.

Statistics and data

In math, pieces of information are known as **data**. Data can be numbers, such as a list of exam results, or words, such as a set of answers to survey questions. Collecting and analyzing all kinds of data is what statistics is all about.

What do you want to know?

One key point of statistics is to find out answers to questions. This can range from scientific questions such as 'How big is a male penguin?' to political questions such as 'What party will people vote for?'.

Taking a sample

To find the answer to questions like these, you need to collect lots of data. But it would take far too long to measure every single penguin, or ask every single person how they will vote. Instead, you can just examine a sample – a small group chosen to represent the whole.

Star math

One of the first great statisticians was French astronomer Pierre-Simon Laplace.

He spent years watching the stars and planets, and measuring the way their path through the sky changed over time. Each year he gained more data, making his analysis more and more accurate.

The biggest sample

One of the first really big surveys took place in Sweden in 1749. The government wanted to find out how many people lived in the whole country.

They expected the answer to be close to 20 million people, but in fact there were just over 13 million.

Nowadays, most governments conduct this kind of country-wide survey, called a census, every ten years or so. The data also helps them decide if the country needs more resources such as schools or more roads.

Together, all the penguins in this colony are described as the **population**.

We're just a sample.

Choosing the sample

It's vitally important to choose a 'good' sample. Two 'bad' samples taken from the same population can give very different results.

For example, a school survey that asks 'How much time is there for sports?' might get the answer 'too much' if the sample was taken from just the chess club, and 'too little' if the sample was taken from the football team. Choosing a specific sample to get a particular result is called **bias**.

8 out of 10 cats prefer soft Cat-i-Bit biscuits to hard Cat-o-Crunch.

But most of the cats in the survey had toothaches, so of course they didn't like the hard biscuits.

Random samples

One way to avoid bias in a survey is to choose a sample at **random**. A random sample means every person from a population has an equal chance of being picked.

For example, you could pick a sample of people waiting to buy movie tickets by putting on a blindfold and pointing at just a few of them.

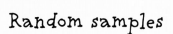

Sometimes a *completely* random sample can be misleading, too. If the movie survey was intended to find out about *all* movie-goers, a sample that only picked out people who are paying for tickets wouldn't represent the views of, for example, young children whose parents buy their tickets for them.

A good sample needs to give a fair representation of the whole population, as well as being random.

The wrong result

In the USA in 1936, a magazine conducted a telephone survey of 10 million people, chosen at random, to ask who they thought would win the Presidential election that year.

The survey showed readers thought Landon would defeat his rival Roosevelt by 370 votes to 171.

But in the actual election, Roosevelt won by 523 to 8.

Why did they get it so wrong? The reason was that in 1936, only wealthy people owned telephones. And most of them wanted Landon to win. So the survey was biased, even though it seemed to be random.

Difficulties with data

The ever-changing kilogram

The Bureau of International Weights and Measures in France holds a cylinder of metal that weighs exactly one kilogram. Traditionally, the most accurate sets of weighing scales were calibrated using this cylinder.

But there's a problem – the metal is slowly disintegrating, losing tiny, tiny amounts of weight over time, so any new scales calibrated using the cylinder will vary slightly from older scales.

Imagine two pirates, Nancy and Jonah, are arguing about who has the most gold. It should be simple to settle the argument, shouldn't it?

I've got 9 gold bars.

I've got 9 bars, too.

All the bars look the same. But when they put their bars on a set of scales to weigh them, Nancy's weigh more than Jonah's.

Ha! I've got the most gold.

Jonah complains, so they weigh the gold again, using a different set of scales. This time, the scales tip the other way: it seems that Jonah's gold weighs more.

How can this happen? The fact is, no two bars of gold are ever exactly alike in size or even purity, and no set of scales is entirely reliable. (In fact, Jonah cheated in the second attempt by putting a heavier bowl on his side of the scales.) But even two modern digital scales can give different readings when weighing the same object.

The best way to be fair is to weigh the bars many times on many sets of scales. Then, compare *all* the results to see if one set comes out weighing more overall.

The more data, the more reliable and more accurate the result.

68

The meaning of average

In everyday use, the word 'average' means just 'ordinary' or 'in the middle'. But in math, there are three different types of averages.

This seed packet contains an 'average' of 23 seeds. But what does that actually tell you?

Avg. contents:
23 seeds

One way to find out is to buy lots of packets and count the seeds in each.

Then put the data into a table, like this:

There are three ways to describe the average number of seeds: **mode**, **median** and **mean**.

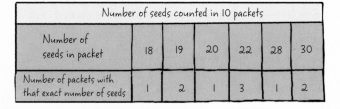

Number of seeds counted in 10 packets						
Number of seeds in packet	18	19	20	22	28	30
Number of packets with that exact number of seeds	1	2	1	3	1	2

The median number of seeds is 22.

The mode number of seeds is 22.

Mean

When people describe an 'average', they are usually talking about the **mean**. It's the value obtained when data is shared out equally.

To calculate it, add up all the results, then divide by the total number of examples (here, the total number of seeds divided by the total number of packets.)

Median

The **median** is the middle number for an odd set of numbers in order, and the average of the middle two numbers (when in order) of an even set of numbers.

30
30
28
22
22
22
20
19
19
18

Mode

The number that appears most often in a set of numbers is called the **mode**. This is one kind of 'average'.

The mean number of seeds is 23. It's still an average, even though no packet in this sample had exactly 23 seeds.

Charting data

Sometimes the easiest way to make sense of data is to draw a chart. There are a number of different ways to do this.

Line chart

Line charts are good for showing how something changes over time.

Each axis needs a clear label.

Speed of a car on a journey

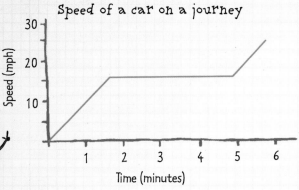

Bar chart

Bar charts are good for comparing the quantities of different things.

Results of a fruit survey at a supermarket

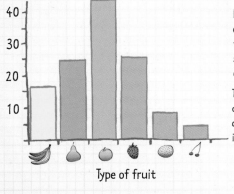

Bar charts only work for **discrete** data – data that can be divided into separate items, such as different fruits.

The bars on a bar chart are the same width, and can have a gap in between.

Histogram

Histograms use bars to compare different samples from a set of **continuous** data – data that can be described as any value within a given range, or interval.

Time taken to finish a puzzle

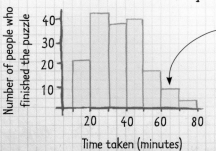

This bar on the histogram shows anyone who completed the puzzle in at least 60 minutes, but less than 70 minutes.

Pie chart

Pie charts use a circle to represent the whole sample. They're useful for showing how different sections of that sample are split up.

How Finn spends his allowance

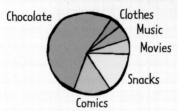

Chocolate

Clothes
Music
Movies
Snacks
Comics

How Poppy spends her allowance

Magazines
Chocolate
Makeup
Jewelery
Movies
Clothes

Analysis of class 2B: how tall students are compared with how long their feet are

Scatter diagram

Scatter diagrams show how two different things may or may not relate to each other.

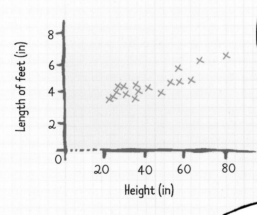

Length of feet (in)

Height (in)

The points on this graph almost fall in a neat line. This suggests there is a link, or **correlation**, between the two factors.

Analysis of class 2B: how tall students are and how well they did in a math test

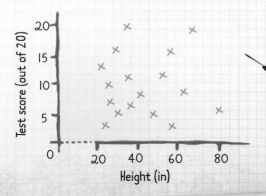

Test score (out of 20)

Height (in)

The points on this graph don't show any pattern. This suggests there is no correlation between the two factors.

Cheating with charts

Sometimes people design a chart in a way
that is intended to mislead readers.

Line chart cheat

This line chart looks very
dramatic, but the data says
otherwise. Look closely at
the numbers...

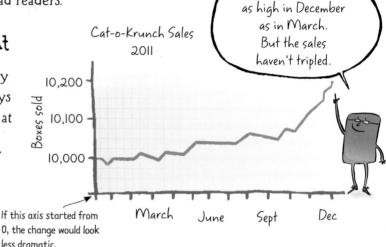

Cat-o-Krunch Sales
2011

The line is three times
as high in December
as in March.
But the sales
haven't tripled.

Boxes sold

10,200

10,100

10,000

March   June   Sept   Dec

If this axis started from
0, the change would look
less dramatic.

Picture cheat

This picture compares the amount
of apples coming from two
orchards. Orchard B produces $1\frac{1}{2}$
times as many apples.

Orchard A   Orchard B

The second apple is $1\frac{1}{2}$
times as long and $1\frac{1}{2}$ as wide as
the first. But this makes it look
more than twice as big overall.

Bar chart cheat

This bar chart compares the subjects
children like at a school.

Some bars are wider
than others, so it
looks as if they are
more popular.

Number who like subject

16
14
12
10
8
6
4
2

English   Chemistry   History   Art

Subject

False correlation

Sometimes a chart seems to show a correlation between two factors. But, just because there's a link, it doesn't always mean one thing *causes* the other. There might be another, hidden, factor. Look at this scatter chart:

Beware!

A single chart is not enough to prove one factor is the direct cause of an event.

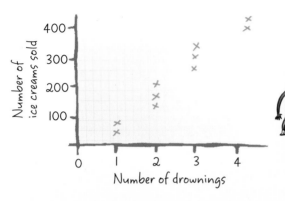

When it's hot, more people eat ice cream, and more people go swimming (so risk drowning). *Weather* is the hidden factor.

Good game, bad game

Data tables can record a range of results over a period of time. They nearly always show the same trend: results tend to average out over time. For example, this chart shows how many goals a kicker scored in every soccer match in a season.

Match	1	2	3	4	5	6	7	8	9
No. of goals	1	2	1	0	4	3	1	0	2

The mean number of goals was approximately 1.5. If you look at the results in sequence, a pattern emerges: a high-scoring game is followed by a lower-scoring game, and a low-scoring game is usually followed by a higher-scoring one.

This pattern is called **regression to the mean**. It shows that, over time, results don't get steadily better or worse, but tend to settle around a mean point.

Praise or punish?

Teachers at a flight school found when they punished a pilot who had just performed badly in a test, he improved next time.

When they praised a pilot who performed well, that pilot did worse the next time.

So the teachers began to punish all the pilots all the time, in the hope of improving everyone's test scores. But it didn't work.

Why not? Because pilots who do badly at one test tend to do better next time, while pilots who do really well tend to do worse, *regardless of praise or punishment.*

In fact, over time, a pilot's scores won't keep getting better (or keep getting worse). The score will settle closer and closer to a mean value.

The average man

Belgian statistician Adolphe Quetelet was one of the first to collect data about people. He wrote a book called *Treatise on Man* in which he used data to describe the height, weight and other characteristics of an average 19th-century man.

The average criminal

Quetelet also collected data about crimes and the people who committed them. His data suggested that criminals were more likely to come from poor homes, have little education, and be drunk when they committed their crimes.

What is normal?

One reason people look at data is to find out what is typical. For example, how big is a typical pumpkin?

A chart that shows data to answer questions like these is called a **distribution chart**, because it shows how a **range** of results is distributed. Distribution charts often show a symmetrical pattern with a peak in the middle, which corresponds to the mean, median and mode.

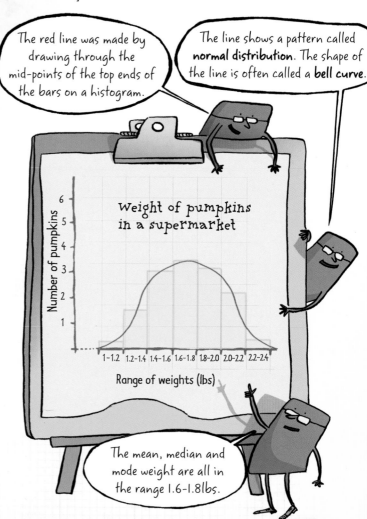

The red line was made by drawing through the mid-points of the top ends of the bars on a histogram.

The line shows a pattern called **normal distribution**. The shape of the line is often called a **bell curve**.

Weight of pumpkins in a supermarket

Number of pumpkins

6
5
4
3
2
1

1–1.2 1.2–1.4 1.4–1.6 1.6–1.8 1.8–2.0 2.0–2.2 2.2–2.4

Range of weights (lbs)

The mean, median and mode weight are all in the range 1.6–1.8lbs.

Standard deviation

It's easy to see a clear mean on a normal distribution chart. But what the chart also shows is by how much a range of pumpkins *vary* from the mean.

There is a point on the line on either side of the peak where the curve stops getting steeper. Nearly two-thirds of the data falls in between these two points. Statisticians describe each point as being one **standard deviation** from the mean.

It's a mathematical way to describe how typical, or untypical, a particular pumpkin is. Most pumpkins differ by less than one standard deviation, but a few tiny or huge ones might differ by three or more.

Uneven distribution

But there are many charts that don't show normal distribution. For example, look at this chart showing how much money people earn:

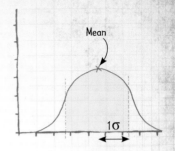

The shaded area on this graph covers two standard deviations from the mean. The symbol σ, sigma, is used as a shorthand for the term 'standard deviation'.

Business standard

Manufacturers, banks and even governments try to improve their performance using a measure known as 6σ, or 'six sigma'.

For example, a company will carefully analyze any product they make that falls six standard deviations below the mean quality level. This helps them ensure the mistakes involved in making the inferior product are not repeated.

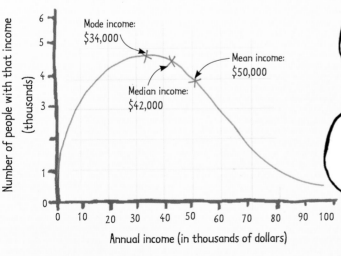

Income of people on Free Market Island

Politicians who want to show how wealthy most islanders are might point to the mean income.

Workers who want to show that they deserve better pay might point to the mode income to prove their point.

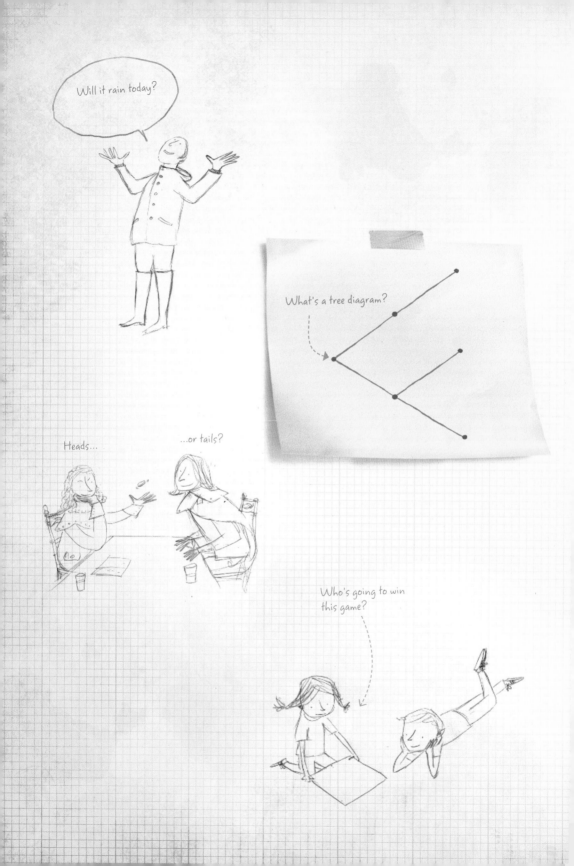

Part 5:
Take a chance

Probability is a branch of math that uses logic and arithmetic to analyze how likely something is to happen. It can apply to anything, from guessing which way to turn in a maze, to deciding whether to bring an umbrella with you on a walk.

Most people talk about probability without thinking about the math behind it. But some people, such as insurance agents, think about it very carefully. For example, to calculate life insurance costs, an agent has to figure out an accurate probability for how long a person is likely to live. This is based on things such as that person's age, health and profession.

The weather forecast is a prediction about what the weather will be like over the next few days.

Weather stations use computers to make calculations, based on measurements of temperature, air pressure and other factors, then compare them with data going back decades.

Is it likely?

It's impossible to know for certain what will happen in the future, but math can help make good guesses. However, some events have so many factors to account for there's no way to make a good guess. For example, is a journey quicker on foot or by bus?

When was the last time we had this temperature, pressure and humidity?

The bus comes every 5-12 minutes.

The journey usually takes 7 minutes.

I can walk it in 8 minutes.

It'll take me at least 25 minutes.

What if there's a traffic jam?

There was a similar pattern for the week of July 15, 1956. And there was a hurricane the following week.

Oh, okay, we'd better warn people!

Probability scale

In math, a probability is given as a number between 0 and 1 (usually written as a fraction or a decimal), that shows how likely something is to happen. Something that will *definitely* happen has a probability of 1. Something that could *never* happen has a probability of 0.

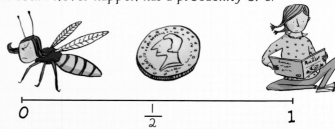

0      $\frac{1}{2}$ 1

You will turn into an insect.

If you toss a coin, it will land heads up.

You will eventually stop reading this book.

Calculating probabilities

To calculate the probability of an event, you need to work out how many ways it's possible for that event to occur, out of the total number of possible outcomes.

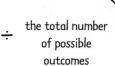

The probability of a particular event, or P(Event) $=$ the number of ways it can happen, *assuming each way has the same chance of occurring* $\div$ the total number of possible outcomes

Monster or not?

Sammy has to choose which way to turn. There are two possible outcomes: meeting a monster or not meeting a monster. He can only go left or right, not backwards, so the probability of meeting one is $1 \div 2$.

$$P(\text{Monster}) = \frac{1}{2}$$

One heart

Lotte selects a card from a deck. What's the probability that she picks a heart?

There are 13 hearts and 52 cards in total. So the probability of picking a heart is $13 \div 52$. Or:

$$P(\text{Heart}) = \frac{13}{52} = \frac{1}{4}$$

Rolling a six

Alex is playing a game using dice, and she wants to roll a six. The dice has six sides, each showing a different number. Assuming it's a fair dice, there are six possible outcomes: 1, 2, 3, 4, 5 or 6. So, the probability that she rolls a six is $1 \div 6$.

$$P(\text{Six}) = \frac{1}{6}$$

It's no harder to roll a six than any other number on the dice. The probability of rolling a six is exactly the same as any other number.

Odd or even?

It's Stefan's turn to roll the dice. What's the probability that he rolls an even number?

There are three ways of rolling an even number: 2, 4 or 6. There are six possible outcomes: 1, 2, 3, 4, 5 or 6. So the probability of rolling an even number is $3 \div 6$.

$$P(\text{Even}) = \frac{3}{6} = \frac{1}{2}$$

Probability trees

When finding the probability of two or more events, it gets a little more complicated. For example, if you toss a coin twice, there are four possible outcomes:

1) heads tails   2) heads heads   3) tails heads   4) tails tails

You can show this in a tree diagram, made up of lines called branches. A new branch is drawn to represent each possible outcome.

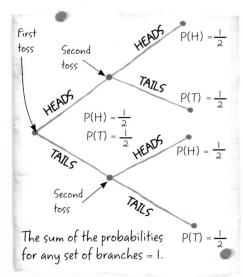

First toss

Second toss

HEADS $P(H) = \frac{1}{2}$

TAILS $P(T) = \frac{1}{2}$

HEADS

$P(H) = \frac{1}{2}$
$P(T) = \frac{1}{2}$

TAILS

Second toss

HEADS $P(H) = \frac{1}{2}$

TAILS $P(T) = \frac{1}{2}$

The probability of getting heads on each toss is always $\frac{1}{2}$, no matter what happened in the previous toss.

The sum of the probabilities for any set of branches = 1.

More events

Even if you've tossed three heads in a row, the probability of tossing heads next time is still $\frac{1}{2}$. But the probability of tossing four heads, *one after another,* is *not* $\frac{1}{2}$. To work this probability out, you need to multiply the probability of each of the four coin tosses.

$P(HHHH) = \frac{1}{2} \times \frac{1}{2} \times \frac{1}{2} \times \frac{1}{2} = \frac{1}{16}$ ← If you drew out the probability tree of four coin tosses, there would be 16 branches at the end.

The key to success

Many card games involve decisions based on probability. People who play a lot often become very good at calculating probabilities in their heads.

For example, the key to winning many card games depends on knowing how likely it is that a certain card will come up on the next turn.

All adding up

When making calculations with probability, it helps to remember the rule:

> The sum of the probabilities of all possible outcomes = 1

For example, when tossing a coin, the probability of getting heads = $\frac{1}{2}$ and of getting tails = $\frac{1}{2}$

$$P(H) + P(T) = \frac{1}{2} + \frac{1}{2} = 1$$

The probability of me winning or you winning is 1!

The problem of points

In the 17th century, two French mathematicians, Blaise Pascal and Pierre de Fermat, became fascinated by probability. They kept writing letters to each other about a particular question they called the 'problem of points'.

PASCAL AND FERMAT IMAGINE THEY ARE IN A CAFÉ PLAYING A COIN-TOSSING GAME...

IF THE COIN COMES UP HEADS, PASCAL GETS A POINT. IF IT COMES UP TAILS, FERMAT GETS A POINT. THE PLAYERS ADD FOUR COINS TO A POT ON EACH TURN. THE FIRST PLAYER TO 4 POINTS WINS THE POT OF COINS.

PASCAL IS WINNING 3 POINTS TO 2...

...WHEN FERMAT SUDDENLY HAS TO LEAVE BEFORE THE GAME FINISHES. HOW SHOULD THEY DIVIDE THE POT?

PASCAL AND FERMAT AGREE THAT PASCAL SHOULD GET A BIGGER SHARE, BUT THEY WANT TO DECIDE EXACTLY HOW MUCH BIGGER.

I'm winning! Maybe I should get the whole pot?

THEY FIGURE OUT ALL THE POSSIBLE WAYS THE GAME COULD HAVE ENDED, USING A TREE DIAGRAM:

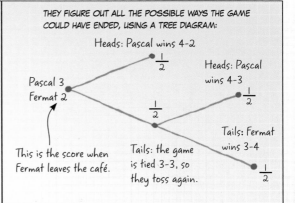

Heads: Pascal wins 4-2

$\frac{1}{2}$

Heads: Pascal wins 4-3 $\frac{1}{2}$

Pascal 3 Fermat 2

$\frac{1}{2}$

Tails: Fermat wins 3-4

This is the score when Fermat leaves the café.

Tails: the game is tied 3-3, so they toss again.

$\frac{1}{2}$

PASCAL AND FERMAT DESCRIBE TWO DIFFERENT WAYS TO SETTLE THE ARGUMENT:

A) The probability tree shows there are three possible outcomes to the game.
  In two of them, Pascal wins.
  In one of them, Fermat wins.
So they could split the winnings 2:1

B) By figuring out the actual probabilities of each of the three outcomes, they found that Pascal has a $\frac{3}{4}$ chance of winning, while Fermat has only a $\frac{1}{4}$ chance.

IN THE END, THEY DECIDE OPTION B) IS THE MOST ACCURATE, SO THEY AGREE THEY WOULD SPLIT THE WINNINGS 3:1.

THE STUDY OF PROBABILITY AS A WHOLE NEW FIELD OF MATH WAS INSPIRED BY THIS CASUAL DISCUSSION OF AN IMAGINARY GAME.

Surveys and estimates

Some probabilities are exact – for example, the probability of picking a red ball from a bag that contains 8 red balls and 2 green balls $= \frac{8}{10} = \frac{4}{5}$.

But not *all* probabilities are exact. Some are just estimates based on an experiment or survey. In a survey, the estimated probability is also known as the **relative frequency**. This is the number of times an event occurs, divided by the total number of trials or observations.

Car count

Here's an example: Lily stands by the road counting how many cars have just one person inside.

Out of ten cars, she notes that seven have a single person inside. When she extends her survey to 100 cars she counts 63 single-person cars. And out of 1,000 cars, she counts 602.

In the first case, the relative frequency of cars containing just one person is $\frac{7}{10}$ or 70%. In the second survey, it's $\frac{63}{100}$ or 63%, and in the third, it's $\frac{602}{1000}$ or 60.2%.

The most accurate result is the one based on the greatest number of observations.

1. 70% 2. 63% 3. 60.2%

To make a general statement about cars and passengers, this result is best.

Frequency charts

Sometimes the best way to understand a survey is to show it clearly in a diagram, such as a **frequency chart**.

Survey: 1,000 children were asked to name a tasty treat.

No. of children

Strawberry spirals · Chocolate mice · Lemon chews · Rocket fizzlers · Kola bears

Treats named

From this chart, you can see that strawberry spirals were the most popular. The relative frequency of a child picking strawberry spirals is about $\frac{650}{1000}$, which is the same as 65%.

Making plans

If you know the relative frequency of an event, it can help to make plans for the future. For example, Nadine was given some new sandals for her birthday on June 1st. But she can only wear them on sunny days. How often can she expect to wear them in June?

1. The calendar tells her there are 30 days in June.

JUNE

2. A website about weather tells her the relative frequency of rainy days in June in her town is 0.4

Expected number of days of rain = 0.4 x 30 = 12

Expected number of sunny days = 30 – 12 = 18

So, Nadine can expect to be able to wear her new sandals on about 18 days in June.

Surprising results

Lucy and Eric have two children. At least one is a boy. What's the probability that the other child is a girl?

$\frac{1}{2}$?

Actually, it's $\frac{2}{3}$.

To find out why, make a list of all the possible pairs of children:

BB, BG, GB, G̶G̶

Since you know one child is a boy, you can rule out the last one. Of the three remaining outcomes, two of them have a girl, so the probability that the other child is a girl is $\frac{2}{3}$.

As you get more information, you can predict an answer more accurately.

Mind reading

Ask a friend to think of a number between 1 and 10. It should be impossible to guess what they'll say with more than 10% accuracy. But if you guess 7, you'll be right about 30% of the time. No one knows why, but surveys around the world show that about one third of people always think of the number 7.

7

Who invented zero?

Why do scientists need to use math?

What does math have to do with music?

Part 6:
More about math

In this section, you can find out how the study of mathematics has developed since the dawn of human history, and discover some of the ways in which math plays a part in working life, and especially in music.

Math through the ages

Ancient scratches on bones show that people have been recording numbers for at least 35,000 years. Since then, math has helped people solve everyday problems, and scholars have invented many new mathematical ideas.

about 4,500 years ago

Ancient Babylonians are writing arithmetic problems on clay tablets – some of the oldest known examples of math.

about 3,500 years ago

An ancient Egyptian text known as the *Rhind Papyrus* poses problems about fractions, prime numbers, geometry and algebra – and tells the reader how to solve them.

about 2,500 years ago

Thales works out how to find the height of a pyramid without climbing it, and Pythagoras studies triangles and irrational numbers.

about 2,300 years ago

Euclid sets out the rules of geometry in his book *Elements*, Archimedes works out π, and Eratosthenes estimates the circumference of the earth.

3rd century

Diophantus is one of the first mathematicians to write problems down using symbols instead of words.

4th century

Hypatia, a Greek scholar living in Egypt, studies Euclid and Diophantus, and creates accurate star charts.

6th century

Chinese mathematician Zu Chongzhi works out the length of a year, and calculates π to 7 d.p. – the most accurate version known for the next 1,000 years.

7th century

In India, Brahmagupta is the first person to use zero to write large numbers, and to show how to use negative numbers.

9th century

al-Khwarizmi writes a book about algebra. Meanwhile, his teacher, al-Kindi, writes four books explaining how to use Hindu-Arabic numerals.

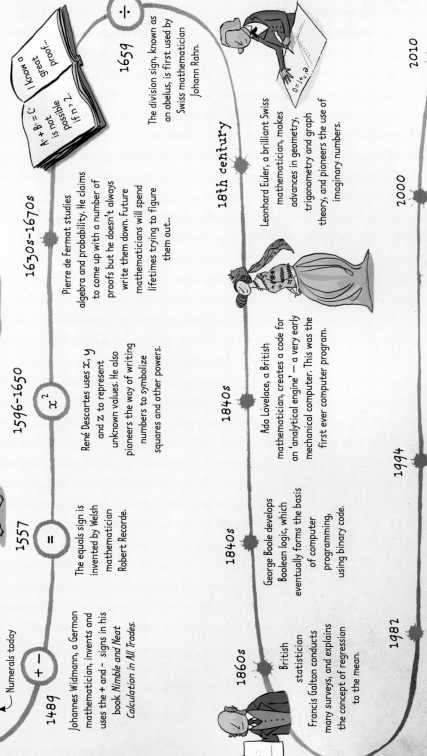

9 8 7 6 5 4 3 2 1
← Numerals today

1489

Johannes Widmann, a German mathematician, invents and uses the + and − signs in his book *Nimble and Neat Calculation in All Trades.*

=

1557

The equals sign is invented by Welsh mathematician Robert Recorde.

x^2

1596-1650

René Descartes uses x, y and z to represent unknown values. He also pioneers the way of writing numbers to symbolize squares and other powers.

1630s-1670s

Pierre de Fermat studies algebra and probability. He claims to come up with a number of proofs but he doesn't always write them down. Future mathematicians will spend lifetimes trying to figure them out...

I know a great proof...

$A^n + B^n = C^n$ is not possible if $n > 2$.

÷

1659

The division sign, known as an obelus, is first used by Swiss mathematician Johann Rahn.

18th century

Leonhard Euler, a brilliant Swiss mathematician, makes advances in geometry, trigonometry and graph theory, and pioneers the use of imaginary numbers.

$0 = 1 + e^{i\pi}$

1840s

Ada Lovelace, a British mathematician, creates a code for an 'analytical engine' — a very early mechanical computer. This was the first ever computer program.

1840s

George Boole develops Boolean logic, which eventually forms the basis of computer programming, using binary code.

1860s

British statistician Francis Galton conducts many surveys, and explains the concept of regression to the mean.

1982

Benoît Mandlebrot publishes *The Fractal Geometry of Nature.* He explains that everything from coastlines to changing stock market prices can be examined as fractals.

1994

The last of Fermat's unsolved theorems is finally solved by British mathematician Andrew Wiles, after 40 years of study.

2000

The Clay Mathematics Institute sets out seven unsolved math problems, and offers a prize of $1,000,000 to anyone who solves one.

2010

Russian mathematician Grigori Perelman solves one of the Clay problems, but turns down the prize money.

Math at work

Nearly every job requires some kind of math, such as simple arithmetic. But some jobs require more complex kinds of math, too.

Entrepreneurs

People setting up a business often need to borrow cash from investors. To convince people to loan them money, they create a business plan using charts and percentages. These describe how much money the business needs, and how much the investors could make in profit.

Scientists

All scientists use math to plan experiments and examine the results. Many kinds of scientists need math for other things, too.

Doctors use ratios to work out a dose of medicine. Ecologists and marine biologists use statistics and graphs to analyze animal populations. Chemists use algebra to figure out the amounts of compounds they need to make a chemical reaction work.

Fashion designers

Fashion designers usually start with a sketch. But to turn that into a piece of clothing, they have to know how to draw the shape they want as a net. They then need to convert the net into a life-size pattern, using measurements and scale, so that when the fabric is cut it's the perfect size and shape.

Stockbrokers

Stockbrokers analyze data and charts relating to stock prices. They try to buy when the stock price is low, and hope that the price will increase, so they can sell their stocks at a higher price to make a profit for their clients.

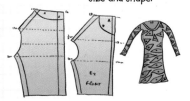

Builders

Builders need to be skilled at geometry so they can turn a plan into an actual building. They also do a lot of estimating volumes and areas, to work out how much of each building material they'll need, how long the job will take to complete, and how many people to hire.

Math in music

When musicians write music, it's like a language, but a language based on math, not words. Music is made up of sounds, called notes, that can be written down as symbols on a set of lines, called a score. The position of each symbol tells you which note it is. The kind of symbol used for each note describes how long to play it for.

A music score

This means there are four quarter note beats in each bar.

A quarter note

A half note is two quarter notes long.

A whole note is four quarter notes long.

How long is a piece of string?

Ancient Greek mathematician Pythagoras made a brilliant discovery over 2,500 years ago: notes that sound good together, that are in harmony, are related mathematically.

Pythagoras also found the sound of a note plucked on a string depends on the length and tension of the string. He plucked a string to make a sound. Then he halved the length of the string and plucked it again, and found the sound it made was almost the same, but a higher pitch. The interval between these notes is now known as an octave.

Bach and harmony

A **chord** is two or more notes played at the same time, to create a harmony. 300 years ago, German composer Johann Sebastian Bach tried out many chords. He ended many of his keyboard-based pieces with a particular three-note chord called a major triad.

Score showing one kind of major triad

A major triad can be defined mathematically, according to the spacing of the notes. Two adjacent notes are exactly one semitone apart. In a major triad, the second note is exactly four semitones above the first, and the third note is three semitones above the second.

Glossary

Words in *italics* have their own separate entries.

algebra The mathematics of using symbols to represent unknowns and to create general rules.

arithmetic Solving math problems using addition, subtraction, mulipilication and division.

average In math, the average value from a set of values is its *mean*, *median* or *mode*.

axis (of a *graph*) A horizontal or vertical line to help define the location of points called *coordinates*. The plural of axis is axes (pronounced ax-eez).

base number The large number in scientific notation form. It tells what number should be multiplied to the *power*.

bias An influence that prevents a *survey* from accurately representing a whole *population*.

binary A system of counting that only uses 1s and 0s. Used by computers to store information.

chart A visual representation of mathematical *data*.

circumference The *perimeter* of a circle.

congruent shapes Shapes that are exactly the same.

coordinates Numbers that define points on a map or *graph* relative to a base line called an *axis*.

correlation A link between two things. One thing may or may not be the cause of the other.

cube root The opposite of *cubing* a number. A cube root is a number that when cubed equals the initial number.

cubing Raising a number to the power 3, which means multiplying three groups of that number.

data Information, such as the results of a *survey*.

decimal place A *digit's* position after a *decimal point*.

decimal point A point used in the *decimal system* of counting. Each digit after the decimal point stands for a tenth, hundredth, thousandth, etc. of one.

decimal system A counting system based on tens.

denominator The number below the line in a *fraction*.

digit Any of the ten Hindu-Arabic *numerals* 0-9.

dimensions The directions in which an object spreads out. A line has one dimension, a square has two and a cube has three.

elevation A drawing that shows the shape of a building seen directly from the front, back or side.

equation A mathematical statement that two *expressions* have the same value.

estimation An approximate answer to a math problem, often found using rounded numbers.

expression A group of symbols, sometimes including *digits*, representing a number in *algebra*.

factors A number's factors are the whole numbers that divide exactly into it.

formula In *algebra*, a rule that explains how a *sequence* is generated, or describes how two or more *variables* are related.

fractal A shape or pattern that repeats itself forever. It exhibits self-similarity, looking the same when you enlarge it.

fraction A number usually written in the form $\frac{a}{b}$ that compares part of an object with the whole. Fractions can also include whole numbers, e.g. $\frac{3}{1}$.

geometry The study of shapes and measurement.

gradient see *slope*.

graph A drawing that shows the relationship between two or more sets of numbers, or between values in an algebraic *equation*.

guesstimate A very rough calculation, made using some numbers that can only be guessed at.

imaginary number A number that doesn't appear on a *real number* line, such as i,$\sqrt{-1}$.

improper fraction A *fraction* with a larger *numerator* than *denominator*, e.g. $\frac{5}{4}$.

infinity An impossibly high number. No matter how high you count you can always go higher, so you can never actually reach infinity.

irrational number A number that can't be written as a *fraction*. In decimal form it has an *infinite* number of *decimal places*.

irregular In *geometry*, a shape that has unequal sides and angles.

linear equation An *equation* that can be depicted on a *graph* using a straight line.

mean One kind of average of a *sample*, found by adding all the numbers and dividing by the total amount of numbers in the *sample*.

median When a set of values is listed in order, this is the value, or values, halfway along the list.

mixed number A number expressed as a whole number with a *proper fraction*, e.g. $1\frac{1}{5}$.

mode The value or item that appears most often in a *sample*.

model A scaled down or simplified representation of a larger or more complex object or situation.

natural numbers Counting numbers, or whole numbers from one upward.

negative numbers Numbers less than zero.

net An unfolded 3-D shape, a flattened cut-out that will fold up exactly to form a 3-D shape.

numeral A symbol used to represent a number.

numerator The number above the line in a *fraction*.

order of magnitude An object that is 10 times bigger than another is bigger by one order of magnitude.

paradox A set of statements that are all true, but also contradict each other.

parallel Parallel lines run side by side and go in the same direction, but never meet.

percentage A type of *fraction*. A whole is 100%.

perfect number A number where, if you add up all its *factors* (except for itself), you get the original number, e.g. 6 is a perfect number because 1+2+3=6.

perimeter The distance around the edge of a shape.

plan A drawing that shows what a shape or building looks like from above.

population An entire group being analyzed in a *survey*, for example, all people living in America.

power The tiny number in scientific notation. It tells you how many groups of the base should be multiplied together.

prime number A number that has only two *factors* – itself and one.

probability The likelihood of an event occurring, described in math on a scale from 0 to 1.

proper fraction A *fraction* with a smaller *numerator* than *denominator*, e.g. $\frac{4}{5}$.

quadratic equation An equation that includes x^2, and no higher power of x.

radius The distance from the center of a circle to any point on the edge of the circle.

random Without order or sequence.

ratio A relationship between numbers, based on multiplication. Often used to compare amounts.

rational number Any number that can be written as a *fraction*.

real number Any number that is positive, negative or zero, including *rational* and *irrational* numbers but not *infinity* or *imaginary* numbers.

reciprocal The reciprocal of a number is found by dividing 1 by that number. For example, the reciprocal of 5 is $\frac{1}{5}$.

regression to the mean A statistical observation that, over time, the results in a *survey* will tend towards the *mean* value of the whole survey, rather than going steadily up or down.

regular In *geometry*, a shape that has sides of equal length and angles of equal amounts.

relative frequency The number of times a particular event occurs in a *sample* divided by the total number of events in the sample.

sample A set of mathematical *data* found by taking part of a *population*.

scientific notation A way of writing large numbers using a *base number* raised to a *power*.

sequence A list of numbers in order, usually related by a mathematical pattern.

simultaneous equations Two separate *equations* that both describe the same variables.

slope How much a line *graph* stretches up compared to how far it stretches along. Also called *gradient*.

square root The opposite of *squaring* a number. A square root is a number that, when squared, equals the initial number.

squaring Raising a number to the power 2, which means multiplying it by itself.

standard deviation A measure of how much variation from the *mean* there is in a *sample*.

statistics A branch of math that deals with collecting, analyzing and presenting *data*.

substitution Solving *algebra* problems by replacing the unknowns in *equations* with numbers.

survey A mathematical exercise to collect *data*.

tally An early way of counting, making scores on wood or bone to keep track of amounts.

term In *algebra*, part of an *expression* usually made of numbers and letters multiplied together, e.g. $3x$.

tessellation An arrangement of repeating shapes to cover a surface without gaps or overlap.

tesseract The shape a cube would take on if it gained an extra *dimension*. Also called a hypercube.

transformation An alteration to a shape's size, appearance, orientation or position.

triangulation Constructing a network of triangles to map out an area, or to narrow down the location of something within an area.

trigonometry The mathematics of angles and triangles, also relating to waves and circles.

units (i) In relation to measurements, units are standard quantities by which length, mass, volume, and so on, are described.
(ii) In relation to numbers, units are the most basic counting value.

variable Another name for an unknown in an *equation*, or the quantities in a *formula*.

Here you can find out the meaning of the symbols used in this book.

$+$ **addition sign**

$-$ **subtraction sign**

$\times$ **multiplication sign**

$\div$ **division sign**

$=$ **equals sign**

n^2 **squared number** A number multiplied by itself. For example, $2^2 = 2 \times 2 = 4$

n^3 **cubed number** A number multiplied by itself twice. For example $2^3 = 2 \times 2 \times 2 = 8$

$\sqrt{}$ **square root sign** To find a square root means to find a number that, when multiplied by itself, gives the original number. For example, $\sqrt{64} = 8$.

$\sqrt[3]{}$ **cube root sign** To find a cube root means to find a number that, when multiplied by itself twice, gives the original number. For example, $\sqrt[3]{125} = 5$.

% **percent** Another way to say 'out of 100'. For example, 17% is the same as the fraction $\frac{17}{100}$.

x A curly x represents an unknown value, or the horizontal axis on a graph.

y A y represents a second unknown value, or the vertical axis on a graph.

z A z represents a third unknown value, or the third axis on a 3-D graph.

n An n usually represents any particular whole number, as opposed to a variable.

$0.\overline{3}$ A dash above a digit – always after a decimal point – means that digit is repeated forever.

π **pi** A number that defines the relationship between the diameter of a circle and its circumference. Approximate value: 3.14

φ **phi** A number that defines the length of one side of a golden rectangle (see page 59). Approximate value: 1.62

∞ **infinity** A symbol that represents the idea of going on forever.

Answers

Here are the solutions to some of the problems posed throughout the book.

1. Picture sudoku, page 4

This is how the completed sudoku grid looks:

2. Shape sequence, page 42

The next shape in the sequence is:

There are two rules in the sequence:
1. Add two extra sides to each new shape.
2. The shapes change color in sequence, too – from orange to red to green.

3. Tangram, page 53

Here's the solution to fitting all the tangram shapes together to make a large triangle:

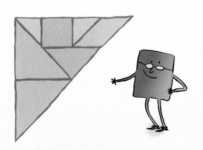

4. Nets, page 59

Here are the matching pairs of 3-D shapes and their nets:

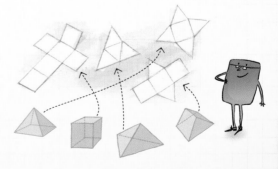

Index

MAY 23 2012

Acknowledgements

Every effort has been made to trace and acknowledge ownership of copyright. If any rights have been omitted, the publishers offer to rectify this in any future editions following notification. The publishers are grateful to the following individuals and organizations for their permission to reproduce material on the following pages (t=top, b=bottom, l=left, r=right)

p44 © Nikreates / Alamy; p49 © Jon Heras / photolibrary.com; p58 © Maximilian Stock Ltd / Science Photo Library (SPL); p59 © Perry Mastrovito / Corbis; p61 (l) © Pasieka / SPL; (r) © ScienceSource / SPL; p62 (t) © B.A.E. Inc. / Alamy, (b) M.C. Escher's "Symmetry Drawing E110" © 2011 The M.C. Escher Company-Holland. All rights reserved. www.mcescher.com; p68 National Physical Laboratory © Crown Copyright / SPL

Art director: Mary Cartwright
Additional design by Steve Wood
Additional illustrations by Steve Wood and Anna Gould
Additional advice from Paul Metcalf